CRE▲TIVE
HOMEOWNER®

design ideas for
Curb Appeal

CREATIVE HOMEOWNER®, Upper Saddle River, New Jersey

CREATIVE
HOMEOWNER®

A Division of Federal Marketing Corp.
Upper Saddle River, NJ

DESIGN IDEAS FOR CURB APPEAL
SENIOR EDITOR: Kathie Robitz
SENIOR DESIGNER: Glee Barre
EDITORIAL ASSISTANTS: Evan Lambert (proofreading),
    Robyn Poplasky (photo research)
INDEXER: Schroeder Indexing Services
FRONT COVER PHOTOGRAPHY: (*top*) Select Home Designs/Bizzo Photography; (*bottom left*)
    Brian Vanden Brink; (*bottom center*) Jessie Walker; (*bottom right*) James Chen
INSIDE FRONT COVER PHOTOGRAPHY: (*top*) Eric Roth; (*bottom*) Anne Gummerson
BACK COVER PHOTOGRAPHY: (*top*) Jessie Walker; (*bottom right*) Stan Sudol/CH;
    (*bottom center*) Roy Inman; (*bottom left*) Jessie Walker
INSIDE BACK COVER PHOTOGRAPHY: courtesy of Malibu
Lighting/Intermatic, Inc.

CREATIVE HOMEOWNER
VP/PUBLISHER: Brian Toolan
VP/EDITORIAL DIRECTOR: Timothy O. Bakke
PRODUCTION MANAGER: Kimberly H. Vivas
ART DIRECTOR: David Geer
MANAGING EDITOR: Fran J. Donegan

Printed in China

Current Printing (last digit)
10 9 8 7 6 5 4 3 2
Design Ideas for Curb Appeal, First Edition
Library of Congress Control Number: 2005931075
ISBN-10: 1-58011-290-0
ISBN-13: 978-1-58011-290-1

CREATIVE HOMEOWNER®
A Division of Federal Marketing Corp.
24 Park Way
Upper Saddle River, NJ 07458
www.creativehomeowner.com

Dedication

For Elisa Miranda—a natural talent when it comes to curb appeal and a variety of other showcasing specialties

Acknowledgments

Thanks to Amy Wax-Orloff of Your Color Source Studios, Inc., and Mark Tirondola of Mark Tirondola Painting Contractor, Inc., for expert advice, and to the McGrails, the Silvers, Joan Manzo, Amy Harrison, Jocelyn Sokol, Tess Giuliani, Sandy Gaul, Kathy Slomin, Nestor Zwyhun, the Gusoffs, and the Esformes, who graciously allowed us to photograph their homes.

Contents

ABOVE A pretty front porch and a freshly painted fence add lots of appeal to this older house.

RIGHT Grouping a few appropriate furniture pieces near the front door looks attractive and welcoming.

BELOW A townhouse appears more approachable with fresh plants and a colorful wreath to soften its brick facade.

A house that has curb appeal gets attention for all the right reasons—and there are many. Handsome design elements, a welcoming entry, great color, and a well-maintained front yard all contribute to its status. You will find excellent examples in *Design Ideas for Curb Appeal.* If you are looking for ways to improve your home's curb appeal, you will be inspired by what you see in the chapters that follow, which examine each of those design elements—and others—in detail. There are ideas for choosing exterior color schemes, creating focal points, adding architectural character, landscaping, and lighting. In addition,

Introduction

you'll find attractive solutions for glamorizing the entry to your house with a new door, unique house numbers, an unusual mailbox, and small accessories with personality-plus. If maintaining a healthy front lawn and garden is frustrating, you can easily rejuvenate the grass using the techniques that are presented here. You'll also find advice on caring for trees and shrubs, as well as six foolproof landscape designs that include a complete list of plantings. Finally, all of these ideas can be tailored to any budget. So get ready to impress your neighbors with your style. Then stand back and say with pride, "That's my house."

Curb appeal—that's a phrase realtors have always used to describe a house that makes a good impression from the street. It's always been a way of saying that the facade and front yard of a house are neat and well-maintained. Today, a house with curb appeal stands apart from its neighbors in terms of creativity, innovation, and charm. It has *presence*. And a property with great curb appeal is not necessarily for sale. If you love your house and are looking for ways to show it, add some color, architectural detail, attractive landscaping, and much more. Let it reflect your own personal style.

What is Curb Appeal?

I pride of place I start with a plan I
I real-life makeovers I
I face value I

Without a doubt the nicest house on the block, this welcoming, well-maintained beauty naturally commands attention.

pride of place

If you gave first-time visitors just the name of your street and not your house number, would they be able to guess which house is yours? Don't be afraid to put your personal stamp on your home's exterior. Begin by looking at the facade and the front yard the way you would look at the interior of your home when you're thinking about making changes. Are you low key with color or do you like to make a splash? Is your style understated? Or do you favor embellishment to draw the eye? How much? Any house can be as personality-rich on the outside as the people who live inside. And it's the attention to those signature details that can transform a basic mailing address into a place you'll proudly call your home. Putting together a plan for making improvements will mean knowing what kind of changes are possible and appropriate for attaining your vision. Architects, designers, landscape architects, and various other professionals and artisans can help you get it right. But first, determine your priorities—including your likes and dislikes and a budget—so that you can communicate them clearly to the experts.

OPPOSITE A meandering stone path and an interesting mix of plantings makes a house on a hill both easily accessible and welcoming.

ABOVE LEFT The time-honored lines of this Tudor Revival house are enhanced by a display of well-groomed ivy and a variegated slate roof.

LEFT Fencing complements the architecture of this house. The porch columns are repeated in the fence posts, and the color is unified.

bright idea

integrity first

A house can be true to
you while remaining true
to its surroundings.
Explore the limits of individual variation that are
still in keeping with
the style of your
house and houses
nearby.

local attraction: ▌▌▌

ABOVE A patio of warmly colored brick pavers and a lush container garden set this
Boston townhouse apart from its nearly identical city neighbors.
▌

OPPOSITE TOP This Hawaiian rancher capitalizes on local color with rooflines,
eaves, and windows that evoke its tropical locale.
▌

RIGHT Adorned with gingerbread trim, the gables of this suburban Virginia Victorian are softened for a look that is more storybook than sharp-edged.
▌

OPPOSITE BOTTOM A crown-molding cornice provides a platform for a small container garden above the entry to a residence in historic, picturesque Newport, R.I.

exterior style should suit the neighborhood...

...and honor original architecture

ABOVE Restoring your home's architectural details is a sure way to add curb appeal. Here, broad timber support beams and trim emphasized in gleaming white paint make this Craftsman Bungalow shine.

LEFT A low stone wall painted in the same rich color as the terra-cotta roofing tiles—the signature feature of an adobe-style house—creates an intimate courtyard. The color is picked up again in the profusion of red blooms.

Colonial

Greek Revival

Gothic Revival

Queen Anne

architectural styles

Italianate Revival

Garrison Colonial Style

Contemporary

Dutch Colonial Revival

Tudor Revival

Craftsman Bungalow

Stick Style

Shingle Style

American Foursquare

Cape Cod Style

Split Level

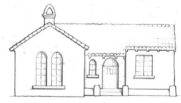

National Style

Spanish Colonial Revival

Ranch

what's your home's curb-appeal quotient?

On a scale of 1 to 10, with 1 being the lowest, what score would you give your house for curb appeal? If it's hard to be objective, perhaps a friend would be willing to give your house a frank appraisal. Of course, if you're planning to sell your house soon, a real estate agent will gladly offer an opinion. Otherwise, go outside, remove your rose-colored glasses, and take a close look. Then, ask yourself these questions:

Is the overall appearance dated? The ubiquitous taupe siding with hunter green trim that was chic in the nineties is kaput. Yes, exterior paint colors, door and window styles, and even certain plantings eventually fall out of fashion. The only exceptions? Strictly period houses, which always look their best when they stay true to their heritage.

Has the house been *mis*improved? Sometimes in an attempt to "update" a house, architectural features may have been obscured or obliterated. It's usually not difficult to restore or add these important details with reproduction or salvaged ornament, moldings, doors, windows, and hardware.

Is the facade tired? Check the siding and roofing for damage or wear. Damaged shingles and shakes are easy to replace; new clapboards are more difficult to install but worth it. You can also repoint eroded mortar joints on brick structures. However, stone and stucco may be more labor-intensive, so you should probably hire a professional to work with you on any related repairs. Don't forget to note peeling paint. Even if you can't afford to paint the entire house, sand and repaint the trim around the windows and doors and the soffits. This minor touch-up refreshes the entire house.

Is the front yard a mess? Kids' toys, overgrown or dead shrubs and grass, weed-ridden garden beds, and debris significantly detract from your home's appearance. Make the kids pick up after themselves; take in the empty garbage cans; and, if you won't do it yourself, hire a lawn service or the teenager next door to mow, rake, and weed regularly. Consider new sod, or at least reseed the brown patches. Replace dead shrubs, or fill in empty areas with annuals.

Is the entry uninviting? Maybe the lighting is poor or the door needs a friendlier color. Sometimes a new mat is all an entry needs to say "welcome."

LEFT A well-landscaped garden that relies on different textures, shapes, colors, and plants of varying height can keep a symmetrical ranch design from looking staid. Windows with divided panes, along with a mix of clapboard and brick exterior surfaces enhance the home's facade.

RIGHT When a house, such as this Queen Anne Victorian, is rich in period detail, maintaining the architectural character may be the best plan.

BELOW Sometimes location will inspire ideas. At this beach house, priority was given to creating comfortable outdoor living space.

As any homeowner who has completed a major renovation will tell you, the success of the project is determined by several factors. The first is the ability of the homeowner to communicate expectations. The research and planning that goes into this stage of the project allows the professionals who become involved later to be precise. The next is finding an architect, landscape designer, or other professional who understands your expectations and needs and who can work within your budget and timeframe. Get references from friends and neighbors who have completed projects that appeal to you. Ask about things like rapport and accessibility. Find out whether they would work with the same person again. Look at online town forums for recommendations. And lastly, make sure contractors have good track records. You can research them in much the same way you research the design professionals. However, most architects and landscape designers routinely work with the same people, so they can often vouch for contractors' and subcontractors' skills and reliability.

start with a plan

design **p**ros

what each one can do for you

▌ **Architects** plan, design, and oversee new construction and major remodels. You will need one if you plan to make any structural changes to the exterior of your house.

▌ **Landscape architects** have extensive formal training in engineering, horticulture, and architectural design. State certification attests to their knowledge about grading and drainage, landscape construction, design, history, and professional ethics.

▌ **Landscape and garden designers** do not need to have formal training. They often work in large nurseries and can help you select appropriate trees, shrubs, and other plantings. They may also provide design advice.

▌ **Landscape contractors** are trained to lay patios and paths, build decks and structures, install irrigation systems, and install plants.

▌ **Paint contractors** provide paint and painting services.

▌ **Siding contractors** sell and install house siding.

OPPOSITE TOP Many interior designers can be helpful regarding decoration. Here, a designer used decorative painting to accent this entry.
▌

OPPOSITE BOTTOM A landscape architect will make certain all design elements are balanced and consistent with the style of the house.
▌

ABOVE A landscape designer can select plants that will thrive in your particular area. This sandy beach soil is no impediment to a perky garden.

real life makeover #1

Once overlooked in a neighborhood of stately tudor and colonial revivals, this small ranch now has presence thanks to a new vaulted entry and roofline.

BEFORE

ABOVE Stately columns and a masonry wall create a focal point. Light filters through the open framework in the entry gable that echoes the look of the home's muntined windows.

BELOW LEFT A lighting fixture with stained-glass panels evokes the Arts and Crafts style, which inspired the renovation.

BELOW CENTER A new oak mission-style front door and sidelight feature a warm wood stain that blends naturally with the earthy green siding.

BELOW RIGHT Decorative metalwork and nature-inspired motifs, such as the dragonfly, reinforce the design theme.

architectural enhancement redefines a 1950s ranch

ABOVE The new entry was moved forward to dramatically change the look of the formerly low-slung ranch.

LEFT Lattice added to the garage wall dresses up the siding and reemphasizes the block pattern over the entry. An eggplant color was used on the shutters to draw more attention to the windows.

RIGHT The homeowners traded small sliding windows for large casement units. Offset by columns and stonework, the new windows, with pop-in muntins that imitate divided lights, form a pattern that is echoed throughout the design.

BEFORE

ABOVE With nearly every element updated, the symmetry and essence of the original house is beautifully reinterpreted.

LEFT Eyebrow cornices above the windows break the roofline, and dentil molding gives this house period detail.

RIGHT The entryway now features a new door and sidelights with leaded-glass panels.

RIGHT The white railing above the entry portico provides a visual balance for the new columns.

BELOW A stone urn adds a sculptural dimension to the garden.

BELOW RIGHT Copperwork above the bay windows will take on a weathered patina as it ages.

lush landscaping and detail romances a colonial

real life makeover #2

With a new landscape design, the house now evokes the feeling of an English country manor in suburban America.

RIGHT TOP The bungalow's original 1913 facade, painstakingly restored, looks onto a busy main street.

OPPOSITE TOP The main entry now faces a quiet cul de sac. A new dormer echoes the lines of the original front gable.

RIGHT CENTER Color accents fine old architectural details.

BELOW LEFT The new door suits the original architecture.

BELOW LEFT CENTER A verdigris finish lends an antique look to a light fixture.

BELOW RIGHT CENTER The lockset is a faithful reproduction.

BELOW RIGHT Windows look like old leaded glass.

OPPOSITE BOTTOM The house numbers and sunburst motif are Craftsman inspired.

BEFORE

BEFORE

a front entrance steps aside to reorient a bungalow

real life
makeover
#3

While updating this vintage house, the homeowner retained the essence of the original architecture of almost a century ago while adding new appeal.

714

The most reliable way to keep your house looking its best—and maintaining its value—is by keeping up appearances. Homeowners who are meticulous about things like keeping the siding and trim clean, masonry in good repair, gutters and downspouts clear, chimneys capped, and roofing updated already have a lot of their curb-appeal bases covered.

face value

Remember, if "clothes make the man," the condition of the exterior of your house says a lot about you to others, as well. Clutter, evidence of disrepair, sloppy window treatments as seen from the outside, and poorly tended yards make a bad first impression. If you're planning an exterior remodel, ask yourself how long you plan to stay before making a large investment. Replacing worn siding or adding outdoor living space will give you the highest financial return, according to most experts, while reroofing may offer the least bang for your buck. A new paint job will probably cost only a few thousand dollars, but it can make your house look like a million. If you're contemplating new landscaping, here's a caveat: in a recent study, 83 percent of realtors said that they believe that homes with mature trees are easier to sell. Finally, don't try to outdo the Joneses; any improvements you make should be in keeping with the neighborhood.

OPPOSITE Routine maintenance keeps this older home in tip-top shape.

ABOVE Furniture that's been freshly painted and given crisp new cushions makes this front porch inviting.

RIGHT A reproduction lighting fixture complements the style of the house.

BELOW Plants and shrubs were selected for their easy care.

Making elements from a few different architectural styles work cohesively can be done successfully if you follow the basic principals of good design, whether you're updating the interior or the exterior spaces of your home.

Start with *scale* and *proportion*. These two principals work together. Scale refers to size. Proportion refers to the relationship of parts or elements based on size. For example, if you're planning to build a covered entry or porch, make sure it's the right size for the existing house. You can apply this principal to landscaping and hardscaping projects as well as to outdoor ornamentation.

Line is another important design element. Give your house more sophistication by incorporating linear interest. Create vertical lines using tall columns, conical trees, or shutters; emphasize horizontal lines with a platform in front of an entrance or a strong balustrade; suggest diagonal lines with with a gabled roofline; and make curved lines using a scalloped flower bed or a curved walkway.

Use your own judgment and good eye to maintain *balance* and *harmony*.

LEFT A gambrel roof on each end of this Dutch colonial home gives it a symmetrical appearance.

ABOVE LEFT An elliptical window balances the off-center entry.

ABOVE TOP Red paint welcomes visitors to the front door.

ABOVE A cylindrical light adds interest.

BELOW The window's oval shape complements the formal facade.

For a dynamic change in the look of your house, no element packs more punch than color, and few design tools are as satisfying to exploit. You can use color in ways that are either subtle or strong. But one thing is for sure: color is always personal. And while there are some guidelines to keep you on track in terms of combining colors and complementing certain architectural styles, the field is usually wide open to your preferences. (Be careful: some localities, especially historic areas, mandate what colors you can paint your house.) Start exploring your options here.

Color and Paint

I how to choose house colors I
I blue I red I yellow I green I earth tones I
I neutrals I paint basics I

This red house really stands out on its wooded lot because the greenery complements the paint color. Note how the roof and chimney stone seem to match.

When it comes to a color, some people find making a choice over-whelming. And indeed, just visiting a paint store and looking at color chips can make you lose perspective. It helps to think about choosing color somewhat scientifically. First, consider your home's location. Because of the absorbent and reflective properties of color, a house that faces south will be exposed to strong sunlight for most of the day, and that will wash out pale colors. Meanwhile, a house that faces north, where the absence of direct sunlight appears cold or even slightly gloomy, can be brightened by warm tones. Eastern esposures are sunny only in the morning; western exposures get lots of light in the afternoon. You can apply these facts to regional color considerations, too. Another influence on your color choice should be neighboring houses. While you may want your house to stand out from the rest, you don't want it to stick out like a sore thumb, either. Don't be a color copycat, but try to blend into the neighborhood by matching the color's *intensity*. If the house next door is a mid-tone blue, avoid pale pastels or deeply saturated versions of any color. Check paint charts in the store, which offer a range of shades and tones in all colors.

how to

choose house colors

OPPOSITE In a rustic setting the rich crimson of this home anchors it into the lush foliage surrounding it. It evokes a warm welcome in the late afternoon sun.

LEFT An older brick townhouse gets a facelift with bright color. Eyebrow arches and sills have been accented in deep red.

ABOVE A color reminiscent of driftwood gives this house by the sea an easy-going air. Black and white accents look crisp.

ABOVE RIGHT Siding painted a verdant green looks lush here. Cream-color trim emphasizes the windows and door.

RIGHT True blue suits this Victorian farmhouse.

color's vocabulary

The following terms are used to identify types of colors or explain their interrelationships.

▌ **Advancing colors:** Warm colors and dark colors, which seem to advance toward you.

▌ **Analogous colors:** Any three colors located next to one another on the color wheel.

▌ **Color scheme:** A group of colors used together to create visual harmony.

▌ **Color wheel:** A circular arrangement of the 12 basic colors that shows how they relate to one another. (See the illustration on this page.)

▌ **Complementary colors:** Colors located opposite one another on the color wheel.

▌ **Contrast:** Using colors with different values and intensities in different proportions to create visual harmony in a color scheme.

▌ **Cool colors:** Greens, blues, and violets.

▌ **Double-split complementary colors:** The colors located on each side of two complementary colors on the color wheel.

▌ **Earth tones:** The neutral colors that dominate in nature.

▌ **Hue:** Synonym for color. Used most often to describe the color family to which a color belongs.

▌ **Intensity:** The brightness or dullness of a color. Also referred to as a color's purity or saturation.

▌ **Intermediate colors:** Red-orange, yellow-orange, yellow-green, blue-green, blue-violet, and red-violet; the six colors made by mixing equal amounts of a primary and secondary color.

▌ **Native colors:** The basic inorganic pigments derived from minerals, used to make the colors found in artist's oil paints.

▌ **Pastel:** A color to which a lot of white has been added to make it very light in value.

▌ **Primary colors:** Red, yellow, and blue; the three colors in the visible spectrum that cannot be broken down into other colors. In various combinations and proportions, they make all other colors.

▌ **Quaternary colors:** Colors made by mixing two tertiary colors.

▌ **Receding colors:** Cool colors and light colors, which make surfaces seem farther from the eye.

▌ **Secondary colors:** Orange, green, and violet; the colors made by mixing equal amounts of two primary colors.

▌ **Shade:** A color to which black has been added to make it darker.

▌ **Split complementary:** A color paired with the colors on each side of its complementary color.

▌ **Tertiary colors:** Colors made by combining two secondary colors.

▌ **Tint:** A color to which white has been added to make it lighter in value.

▌ **Tone:** A color to which gray has been added to change its value.

▌ **Triad:** Any three colors located equidistant from one another on the color wheel.

▌ **Value:** The lightness (tint or pastel) and darkness (shade) of a color.

▌ **Value scale:** A graphic tool used to show the range of values between pure white and true black.

▌ **Warm colors:** Reds, oranges, yellows, and browns.

THE COLOR WHEEL

III accent house architecture with color IIIIIIIIIIIIIIIIIIIIIII

ABOVE LEFT Gleaming white paint draws attention to the traditional stately style of this house and its classic architectural details.

ABOVE Bold black trim outlines the modern shape of this house and ties together its two wings, one subdued in gray and the other painted racy red. Green accents look almost organic.

LEFT Green window trim and natural-color shakes blend beautifully with the trees and stone on the site.

RIGHT A restored Victorian, a proud "painted lady," offers an almost endless canvas for shading, detailing, and combining colors to show off its highly ornamented facade.

make a perfect match

OPPOSITE TOP The natural stone that dominates the ground floor facade suggested the neutral shade chosen for the siding.

ABOVE Choosing a siding color that coordinates with the roof shingles was important because the slope puts much of the roof into into the field of vision here.

Some homeowners prefer an exterior color scheme that coordinates with the palette they've chosen for the interior spaces of their home. However, the best way to determine how your house colors will come together in one perfect palette for all of the exterior elements—the siding, trim, door, shutters, and even the roofing material—is to see them in front of you. If you want to be very high-tech, there are computer programs available that will put all of the colors together for you. But simpler methods are just as effective and a lot more personally satisfying. Draw a sketch of your house, and make several photocopies. Then use colored pencils to add in the details. Later you can get paint chips of all the colors and look at them together, but for an initial overall picture, informal colored sketches work fine.

Most houses will have some fixed features that can help determine the color direction you should take. Look at the roof, for example. Whether it is covered in slate, asphalt shingles, terra-cotta tile, metal, or something else, the roof is a large visible surface, and its color should coordinate with the color of the facade. Unless you plan to paint over brickwork or natural siding, add its color (or a close representation) to your palette. Additional masonry features, such as front stairs, walls, walkways, and driveways, should be accounted for on your sketch, too. And don't overlook the foundation or the foliage. Finally, just as a guideline, put a representative sampling of your neighbors' house colors in the margins of your sketch.

strike a balance with the hues of existing elements

OPPOSITE BOTTOM A slate roof provided the inspiration for painting the brickwork blue. The stucco and accent colors are picked up from the tones present in the walkway.

LEFT The bold blue color used on the foundation is echoed by the shutters.

RIGHT Two strong fixed elements, brickwork and a black roof, are balanced by light yellow siding. The shutters pick up the color of the red brick.

blue

Of all the colors you might paint your house, blue is perhaps the most versatile. Its many shades can range from deeply dramatic navy and cobalt to comfortable midtones, such as cornflower and denim, or whispery pastels like ice blue or Wedgwood. Each suggests different characteristics. Deep slate blue appears formal and solid, while soft robin's-egg blue looks casual or even playful. Muted gray-blues and skylike tints have an American Colonial quality, while green-tinged Prussian blue and delft blue are European-inspired. The one thing all shades of blues have in common is the potential to evoke the soothing qualities of the summer sky and the visual excitement of a shimmering sea. If you choose blue for the facade of your house, take inspiration for the trim or accent colors from the other colors in nature that combine beautifully with those of the sea and sky—cloud white or sandy beige, for example. Blue often partners well with yellow, too, but also stands out with its complement, orange, especially if the latter is softened or deepened rather than fully saturated.

3 **b**lue **l**ooks

Fresh and harmonious, blue color schemes can be varied, such as:

ABOVE AND FAR RIGHT Black and robin's-egg blue temper this daring yet handsome bright blue palette.

ABOVE RIGHT Teal blue looks charmingly vintage with cream-colored accents.

bright idea

blue heaven

Instead of painting a porch ceiling white, paint it sky blue, an old-time tradition that was once thought to keep flies away.

3 red looks

Exuberant and warm, red schemes can be devised in several ways, including:

LEFT Pink with vibrant white trimwork exudes a relaxed charm on this summer cottage.

red

Conventional wisdom says it takes a strong measure of confidence to paint a house red. Once you take that step, you will gain a reputation for extraordinary courage in decorating. But if you think about it, choosing red really isn't as risky as it might seem at first. Red structures are a staple of the American landscape, from the great big barns and silos of farm country to the brick townhouses scattered around every city. One thing is for sure, a red house is sure to gain attention. This stong primary color never looks demure. But because it is so dominant, you may want to avoid pure fire-engine red and look for a shade that's less aggressive, such as crimson, ocher, raspberry, or burgundy. If you're sweet on pastels, consider pink, which is almost a neutral in its palest form. Both red and pink pair pleasingly with complementary greens or neutral hues.

ABOVE Reminiscent of the classic little red schoolhouse, this country home looks ravishing in red with whimsical white trim.

3 yellow looks

Luminous and lighthearted, yellow can be earthy or sharp and bright. The dulled hue has an antique quality, while clearer tints appear more modern. Here are several versions of yellow with possible accent colors:

Yellow can be tricky if it's too bright, but there is a proper shade for any house. Warm and welcoming, yellow glistens in the light of warm climates and provides a hint of sun on wintry days elsewhere. Trimmed in white, yellow looks particularly clean and fresh. But it's equally friendly to a variety of trim and accent colors. Color experts point to it as the most popular house color because it evokes positive emotions. It's also a great choice for homeowners who may be timid about color. Many versions of yellow are mild enough to qualify as neutrals. Such

yellow

shades allow you to use the less intense color for the main body of the house and reserve bold hues for accents.

LEFT This buttery yellow house looks cheerful with pure white trim and hunter green shutters. Because of its yellow tones, green is a natural accent for this hue.

BELOW Blue, especially the warmer shades, provides a fresh contrast—and pleasing balance—to sunny yellow.

bright idea
the right shade

A yellow that is too strong can be overpowering in full sunlight. If in doubt, go with a shade that is less intense than your initial choice.

3 green looks

Natural and revitalizing, green is easy to live with, regardless of the style of your house. Grayed greens, such as sage or moss, have a traditional appeal; bright yellow-greens look more contemporary. Here are a few variations on a green theme:

LEFT Tints of pretty pink flowers in the front garden enhance this spring-fresh house palette.

RIGHT A pale green paint is a safe bet if you're color-shy. It's simply lovely here.

bright idea
nature's cues

Need inspiration? Look at the many shades of green in your garden: bright acidic hues, muted mosses, and deep forest shades.

Green, the most frequently occurring color in nature, is the perfect choice for blending a house with the landscape. As a mix of yellow and blue, green's balance of warm and cool is easy on the eye. In terms of color psychology, green is a safe color that makes people feel satisfied and at ease. And who wouldn't want that feeling embodied by their home? Because green is the perfect complement to red, using shades of green around brickwork often makes a striking arrangement. A pale green is always perfectly accented by a deeper shade of itself, too. Remember, nature mixes greens freely. Just be careful: some blue-greens clash with yellow-greens if they're used in equal amounts.

green

Many people like comfortable, natural earth tones—from shades of the deepest brown to almost-white beige, and even some greens that have been muted with a few dollops of black or brown. Some architectural styles, such as Prairie and Mission, evolved from a philosophy that emphasized the use of natural materials in their naturally occurring states and hues. For this reason, these kinds of houses lend themselves especially to earth tones. So do homes that are built near the coast where sea air is allowed to weather natural shakes and shingles until they become as silver-gray as driftwood. Deep browns need accent color—try picking up red, which is inherent in chestnut brown—to keep it from becoming gloomy. To enliven beige, look to a rosy peach or sandy shades.

earth tones

3 earth **t**one **l**ooks

Comfortable and homey, earth tones go with almost any other color. Keep an earth-tone palette from becoming bland. Here are a few suggestions for subtle combinations:

bright idea

options open

Colors "of the moment" change quickly. So use at least one accent color that is easy to update so that your earthy-tone palette never becomes passé.

ABOVE Earth tones blend beautifully into the natural setting. Here an earthy red door adds just enough zest to invigorate the subtle palette.

RIGHT The concrete on this home's facade was treated with a sophisticated shade of grayish taupe. The white-painted trim makes the color pop.

3 neutral looks

Simple and complex, neutrals are more than black and white. They can be gray-green, khaki, or the color of cooked mushrooms. Here are a few variations:

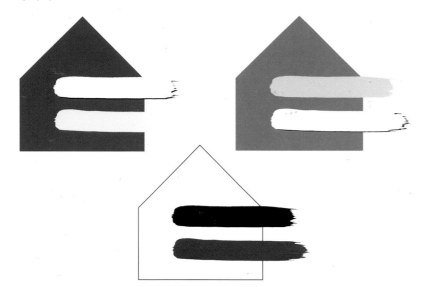

Neutrals—white, black, gray, and sometimes the palest shades of brown—are safe choices that offer a lot of latitude when you're choosing accent colors. White is a popular house color, but it looks especially pleasing with black and paired with classic-inspired architecture, such as Colonial or Federal styles. White is also an excellent choice if one of the fixed colors on your house, such as the roof or the stonework, is outstanding and difficult to match. But keep in mind that white comes in many variations from warm to cool, so it may not be as easy to find the right one as you may think. Gray also presents numerous choices; pale tones can be a sure bet, but dark versions of gray can be too dramatic.

neutrals

bright idea
tone it

While it's a good idea to spark a neutral scheme with at least one accent color, steer clear of very bright shades. The intensity of the accent should equal the intensity of the neutral, or the result can look garish.

OPPOSITE Turquoise accents keep this home from becoming a big white box.

LEFT The reds of the roof and walkway and small touches of strong blue in the tiles, windows, and doors provide the perfect accents for this bright white adobe-style house.

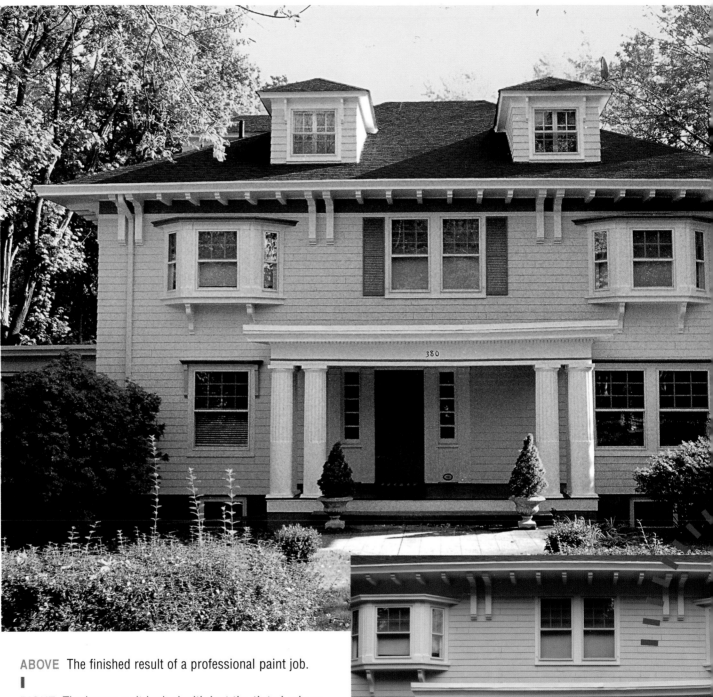

ABOVE The finished result of a professional paint job.

RIGHT The house as it looked with just the tinted primer, which is very close to the final color.

OPPOSITE TOP LEFT Masking and covering windows saves work by eliminating drips that can ruin the finish.

OPPOSITE TOP RIGHT The shake siding as it appeared after stripping.

OPPOSITE BOTTOM RIGHT Labor-intensive stripping on some features, such as dentil molding, can be costly.

paint basics

Whether you decide to paint your house yourself or hire a contractor to do it, it's wise to understand what actually goes into a first-rate job. Good planning and quality paint are key. Latex paint, which is water-based, is usually best. This type of paint is favored because it's very durable, has a short drying time, produces less fumes, and cleans up easily with water. Alkyd paint, which is petroleum-based, has excellent retention and is typically used on house trim. However, it's flammable and must be cleaned up with mineral spirits. Use paint with a flat finish (a nonreflective, matte sheen), which hides imperfections best, for the body of the house and semi- or high-gloss paint for trim, shutters, and doors. It's a good idea to powerwash the siding before painting it. You can have this done professionally or rent the equipment to wash down the siding yourself. Schedule painting over a dry, relatively cool weather period. Pay attention to curing times for the cleaning products, mildew treatments, wood fillers, primers, as well as paints. Also keep in mind that all facets of a house painting project bring you into contact with potentially harmful lead, asbestos, or other harmful chemicals. Sanding and scraping create dust that can be inhaled or get into your eyes. Take the proper precautions: make sure a dust mask, protective glasses, and gloves are part of your supply list, and *use them.*

how to hire a paint contractor

A good paint contractor is recommended by successful examples of his work. Generally, it's best to hire a contractor who is established in the community and is endorsed by satisfied customers. You can also find paint contractors in on-line community forums. Some paint or home-improvement centers will provide a list of painters, too. Before you ask contractors for an estimate, look at examples of their work. Talk to their customers, and find out how satisfied they are with the finished result and the overall experience.

Get estimates in writing from at least three contractors. You need to go over the house with them and discuss any trouble spots and the proposed solutions. How much repair work the job entails will affect the cost. You must understand clearly what materials the contractor intends to use, whether he intends to prime the entire house or spot prime, and how much time the project will take.

A contractor should be licensed and insured, and he should guarantee the work. Find out who will actually carry out the job and whether a supervisor will be on hand at all times. Determine ahead of time the days and hours the painters will work, weather permitting. Also, resolve how and where the clean up and disposal of materials will take place.

I I I I I a good paint job will last at least 10 years I I I I I I I I I I I I

OPPOSITE BOTTOM Painting is every bit as attractive an option for cedar shakes as stain. Here, warm earth tones on the shakes and siding contrast with white windows and doors for a fresh, up-to-date feeling. Warm red accents add just the right amount of saturated color.

RIGHT There is more than one approach to unifying a facade with different siding materials. Here, the homeowners painted the lower brickwork and upper clapboards the same shade of raspberry red.

ABOVE A medium-textured stucco wall is the easiest and fastest exterior surface to paint. Powerwashing can damage stucco, so test in a small area first and use only the lightest setting when you're cleaning it before painting.

RIGHT The deep blue chosen for this house matches the color intensity of the red-tiled roof. White is used as a trim color, all with stunning results.

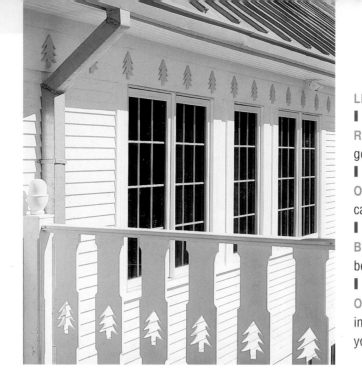

LEFT All-white looks clean and crisp here.

RIGHT This home's cedar shakes have been painted golden yellow to blend with the stone.

OPPOSITE TOP A semitransparent stain gives this cape cod a subtle coat of color.

BELOW A transparent stain reveals the beauty of this beach cottage's naturally weathered shakes.

OPPOSITE BOTTOM Tinted masonry siding features integral color, which means that you have to choose your palette before the material is applied.

paint **v**ersus **s**tain

Whether to paint or stain wood siding is purely an aesthetic choice. Today's latex paints and stains offer the same degree of protection for siding as alkyd-based coatings and, applied properly, will hold up for the same number of years. Working with alkyd-based paints and stains is somewhat more difficult because they require the use of a solvent for cleaning and they are flammable.

If your house has natural-wood siding that you want to show off, you have a few staining options. First, you could use a clear sealant, which has no pigment. Otherwise, to retain the appearance of the wood grain but alter the color, try a semitransparent stain. This product is color-tinted, but just enough so that the grain of the wood is still apparent.

The decision whether to use an opaque stain or a paint must also be based on the condition of the siding. If the siding is new, it's simply a matter of preference. If it's old, you're limited by what's been used previously. If care has been taken with the paint over the years, stripping down to the original wood may be an option. But if wood siding has not been properly treated throughout the years and the grain is interrupted by patches and repairs, a paint is probably the easiest and most sensible choice, because paint tends to hide the grain. Latex paints and stains retain color and look attractive on any type of clapboard.

ABOVE LEFT An antique door, such as this oak beauty, was restored to its original warm honey grain to make a fitting entrance to this grand old house.

ABOVE RIGHT An original stained-glass window was trimmed in a warm cream. It gains added grandeur from gold-leaf accenting.

BELOW The floors and handrails, stripped and stained in hues that complement the age and stature of the house, bring added warmth to the large porch.

ABOVE An old house, rich in architectural detail, wears a meticulous application of new paint and color like a crown. Some of the surfaces, such as the porch floor and ceiling, the stairs, and the porch rail cap, were stained a deep chestnut color to add richness to the wood.

stripping

There are several ways to strip layers of old paint. Chemicals soften the paint so that you can scrape it. A heat gun does the same thing without chemicals. Then there's sandpaper, sharp scrapers, power washers, and more. The trick is to pick the most practical method for your job. On large surfaces, such as the side of a house, applying gallons of caustic chemicals would make a mess and be difficult to handle. Those surfaces should be power washed or scraped. Chemical strippers and heat are better for small jobs, such as removing layers of paint from molding. Where grooves and other details in the wood are almost filled with old paint, you may need several applications. On flat surfaces, you can use a putty knife to clear the softened paint. In tight spots, use a shaped scraper blade. There are hand-held models and tools with interchangeable heads designed to dig into all kinds of beading and channels. Before stripping, be sure that the paint is not lead-based. Have a sample checked if you're uncertain. Also bear in mind that your town may have restrictions on disposing of the waste. If you use a chemical stripper, always wear rubber gloves and a safety mask.

R estoring an old house with paint is particularly satisfying because frequently the detailing on an older home lends itself so well to the project. The best beginning for such an undertaking is to make a thorough assessment of your present paint job. Noting trouble spots and places where the paint has failed will tell you how extensively you need to repair surfaces. Before any new paint is applied, all surfaces must be cleaned thoroughly. To ensure a smooth finish, old crazed, blistered, buckled, or peeling paint must be stripped. Paint that is mildewed or stained by rust must also be stripped. Any underlying wood must be cleaned and primed before proceeding. To ensure that the top coat covers evenly, it's a good idea to prime all areas.

3

When you stop to think about it, you open and close a lot of doors everyday. Few of them are as important as the front door to your home. It is the actual and symbolic separation between the outside world and your personal sanctuary. It's only fitting that this portal is given the attention it deserves—and commands. Also, your home's windows, especially those at the front, allow more than a glimpse out, or into the world inside. They fill an architectural role, helping to define your home. The following pages offer ideas for making the most of your front door and windows' appearance.

Ins and Outs

I grand gestures I
I pathways and front stairs I
I windows I

The front door is an introduction to your home as well as an important security feature. There are many ways to make it welcoming and secure.

If an artist were to render a painting of the front of your house, would the focal point of the artwork be the front door? That's where great curb appeal begins. The front entry should be the first indicator of the kind of style and hospitality one can expect to find inside. There are a variety of practical ways to dress up a front entrance. In terms of improving the look of your house, any time spent on this natural focal point will pay dividends. Besides updating and generally upgrading a house's look, a new front door establishes a specific ar-

grand gestures

chitectural style. It doesn't have to cost a lot, either, depending on the material and various other decorative details. For example, a door with leaded-glass panels will be more expensive. However, embellishing the architecture around a plain door using handsome molding or some other ornamentation will add character, too, and a fresh coat of paint always works wonders. Remember that doors, front stairs, pathways, hardware, house numbers, mailboxes, and screen doors all offer opportunities for creativity and curb appeal. Find your inspiration in the ideas that follow.

ABOVE RIGHT A formal front entry welcomes visitors into this house in a grand way with white-painted wood trim, an oculus, a decorative frieze, an eyebrow arch, corbels, and pilasters.

RIGHT Decorative architectural elements, such as the iron railing and low-relief lintel, draw attention to a double-door entry here. The natural wood finish is understated yet elegant, and its honey tones warm the home's stone facade.

OPPOSITE A porticoe's fluted columns frame a pair of massive wood-paneled doors and dramatize the entrance to this house. The rich dark hue of the doors' finish stands out from the off-white trim and molding of the frame. Complementary door hardware adds gleam.

ABOVE LEFT This painted wood door with louvered panels features a half-moon transom that echoes the doorway arch.

LEFT Sunny yellow paint dresses this charming Dutch door with cheerful color.

ABOVE Here's an example of a country-style door that's been inspired by a European design. The look complements the home's rustic stone facade.

door **s**tyles and **m**aterials

The first consideration for selecting a new front door is style. It's best to choose a design that's consistent with the rest of the house. If your existing door is original to the house, there still may be room for improvement. An updated version of the door will look and function better.

Most entry doors take their design cues from traditional frame-and-panel-constructed wood doors. The most popular exterior door is a *raised-panel* door; the stiles and rails that make up the door frame create an attractive pattern into which the carved or routed panels of the door fit to complete the design. In many doors, glass panels, called *lights* in door-speak, are also included and inserted into the frame as part of the design.

There are countless style variations on the single raised-panel door. Double-door styles are also popular. The advent of energy-efficient glass has given rise to a wide variety of glass doors, too. For the same reason, today's traditional-style raised-panel doors can feature more glass—simple panes or stained- and leaded-glass panels. Sidelights, narrow windows on one or both sides of the door, transoms, and glass panels above the door are frequent options, too. Some manufacturers offer Dutch doors, in which the top and bottom halves of the door can open independently.

Although the look of a traditional door has not changed much over the years, the materials used and the underlying construction have. Of course, a wood door is still an excellent option. It's sturdy and secure. And it can be painted or stained. But a wood door can warp and requires care to keep it looking good and operating well.

Energy-efficient steel and fiberglass are the newest door materials. Because these doors are not wood, they resist shrinking, swelling, and warping. They stand up to extremes of weather and high traffic without scratches and dents. Fiberglass doors have a faux wood grain molded into their finish. Steel doors generally have a flat surface. Both can be painted or stained to look like wood.

RIGHT A traditional raised-panel door is a typical American style. Painted white, this door stands out against the home's cedar-shake siding.

buying and **r**eplacing a **d**oor

Doors are sold prehung (in which case the door is mounted in a frame, sometimes with holes for the lockset predrilled) or as individual components. Unless you have hung a door before, spend the extra money for a prehung unit. It's not that the skills required to assemble a frame and hinge a door are all that difficult, it's the time you'll save. On an exterior door, you will also be assured of a tight weather seal. If you want to replace or upgrade an old door, just buy the door alone and use the original as a template for mounting hinges and the lockset.

Don't count on moving or adding a larger front door in just one afternoon, because there is a lot to the job. First, you have to locate and cut a hole through an existing wall. Then, after you remove the old wall framing, you have to frame the rough opening and install the new door. You'll need good carpentry skills and a building permit in many locales, but the job is within the range of many DIYers.

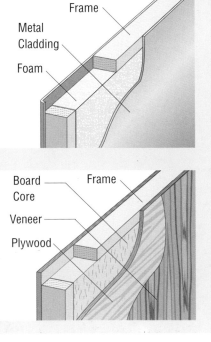

Metal-clad doors are increasingly popular because the metal needs little maintenance and the foam core is energy efficient.

Solid-core doors are used on exterior openings for security and durability. They often need three hinges due to their weight.

bright idea

sidelights

If you have a dark entry foyer, sidelights can improve the look of things inside and out.

BELOW This brightly colored door provides a clue to what visitors will see first when the door is open— an artful staircase.

OPPOSITE TOP LEFT An entry door and storm door made of wood pair well when painted the same color.

ABOVE This front door makes a strong statement, with its dark wood stain, leaded- and stained-glass panels, and wrought-iron hardware, including a door knocker, a reproduction lockset, and oversize strap hinges.

handsome door hardware adds security with distinction

ABOVE LEFT This elegant lockset features a dead bolt integrated with a vintage-style door handle. An antique finish gives it resonance.

ABOVE RIGHT Old World styling sets these knobsets apart from the rest and complements ornately paneled doors.

LEFT Elaborate grillwork displayed in the sidelights and transom coordinate with the substantial hardware on this massive door.

RIGHT An understated lever handle and brass threshold plate add subtle gleaming accents to this design.

locksets

The term lockset describes the entire mechanism of a door handle, whether it locks the door or latches it. A lockset includes the door knob, a latch bolt or locking mechanism, and a decorative plate (escutcheon or rose) that covers the lock mechanism. Latch bolts are spring-loaded and may have a locking mechanism. A dead bolt is not spring-loaded and locks and unlocks only with a key or thumb turn.

Entry-door locks can be locked and unlocked from both sides of the door. One type will lock automatically when the door closes and unlock with a key from the outside or by turning a knob from the inside. For added security, exterior doors are often fitted with a separate dead-bolt lock, located above a door's key-in-knob lockset.

Locksets come in many styles and finishes. Choosing a unique style is an easy way to add individuality to your entryway. When deciding what finish you like, be sure to coordinate with any other metals used in your entry or other parts of your exterior design.

bright idea

technology knocks

PIN security has arrived at your front door. This battery-driven bolt lock lets you program a security code so you can use a key or punch in without one. Change the code whenever you like. An alarm sounds after three wrong entries. A low-battery light helps you keep it up and running.

LEFT These two door knockers share a satin nickel finish but could not be more distinct from each other. The stream-lined look of the far left one is distinctly contempo-rary, while the ornate example near left takes its cue from older European style.

kickplates, knockers, nifty house numbers,

LEFT Proving that the classics never go out of fashion, these time-honored number styles and the traditional polished-brass hardware offset a lovely front entrance.

OPPOSITE TOP Play the numbers to liven things up around the door. Look on-line or in specialty shops for house numbers that are out of the ordinary. Today, it's easy to find numerals, available in vari-ous finishes, to match your home's architec-ture and style.

and mailboxes add personality

where to install house numbers

If you've ever been frustrated searching for an address, you can understand the importance of well-placed, easy-to-read house numbers. Because the entrance is the focal point of the house, placing numbers on or near the front door generally makes sense. (The numbers above were painted on the front door.) If a house is set far back from the street or if there is more than one approach, as may be the case with a corner property, an additional set of numbers may be in order.

Once you've found a spot that seems right, don't be too quick to permanently affix the numbers. Using paper, a marker, and some tape, draw numbers the same height and thickness as the ones you will install. Then temporarily tape them where you think they will look the best and inspect them. Can you properly read the numbers from the street? According to sign-maker specifications, 3-inch numbers should be readable from a distance of 30 to 100 feet; 4-inch numbers should be readable from a distance of 40 to 150 feet. Check to see whether trees or shrubs close to the road obscure the view. Remember that a sharp contrast—dark numbers against a light surface or vice-versa—is best. Lighting at night helps, too.

mailbox makeover

A new mailbox is a must when the old one is too small, damaged somehow, or provides too little security. But by and large mailboxes are sturdy and long lasting. Usually the only problem with an old mailbox is ugliness.

Instead of tossing your tired, weather-beaten metal mailbox, you could target it for improvement. Go over the surface with soapy water; wipe it dry; then lightly sand any rust spots. Before painting, apply a coat of metal primer. Then use acrylic craft paint or paint specially formulated for use on metal. If you want to personalize the mailbox with a design, paint your motif freehand or use stencils. Decals or stickers are another decorating option. Finish with several coats of a clear exterior urethane varnish.

The mailbox post is another item for improvement. Replace a simple post with a more elaborate crossbeam style, and add a decorative post cap or finial. Don't forget to freshen an old post with paint, too. The right plantings situated around the post can add even more charm. Consider low-maintenance grasses and colorful perennials, including flowering vines.

ABOVE The Victorian styling and faux patina of this mailbox make it a perfect fit with the older home it serves.

RIGHT Something as simple as star cutouts across this ordinary gate distinguish it from others and draw attention to the house numbers on the post.

bright idea

dig this

Before you set to work with a spade or post-hole digger, call your utilities company to check for underground lines. Also, a mailbox must be 42 inches off the ground and 2 feet from the side of the road to allow the mail carrier to clear traffic.

LEFT A gleaming white mailbox and a house-number plaque stand out amid a bed of multicolored lilies.

ABOVE LEFT A pair of evergreens in white box planters, a favorite in formal settings, complements this front door. Brass numbers pop against white siding.

ABOVE RIGHT The addition of a transom extends the height and thus the impact of this entryway. Large house numbers have been painted onto the transom.

BELOW Imagination and a sense of humor led to this three-dimensional mosaic extravaganza, which incorporates numbers with the mailbox.

storm and screen doors

Storm and screen doors provide an added barrier against the elements in winter and allow you to vent the house on warm days. If you have a new fiberglass or steel door that provides a high degree of insulation and a tight seal, a storm door is largely unnecessary. You can still use one to get the screening benefits, but be aware that very strong sun shining through the glass of a storm door can actually damage a new exterior door and weaken weatherstripping.

Storm doors can be made of metal, vinyl, or wood. They range in construction from a simple metal panel with interchangeable glass and screen inserts to complex wood or composite core doors with aluminum or vinyl cladding. In some models, glass and screens slide into place or out of the way within the door on tracks. Others have retractable screens that roll up and out of the way within the door frame. For those who want the benefits of a screen in the summer but don't need a storm door the rest of the year, a retractable screen door is the best option. Most doors have a sweep along the bottom of the door that keeps moisture, dirt, and air from penetrating.

Increasingly, storm-door manufacturers are offering doors in colors. Except for the retractable screen, all storm and screen doors offer some kind of latch. If you are looking for another layer of security from your screen door, consider laminated security glass and a multipoint locking system.

bright idea

now you see it...

Tucked away in a pocket off to the side when not in use, a retractable screen door eliminates the need for a traditional swinging screen door.

ABOVE Storm and screen doors come in numerous styles. Today, many home-owners prefer ones like this model, which doesn't cover up a handsome front door. Some types come with etched or beveled glass inserts that can be replaced with a screen during warm months.

RIGHT This tradi-tional white-painted wooden screen door matches the entry-way trim and blends easily with the overall design of the house.

OPPOSITE Scouring antique shops for something unique, homeowners found these one-of-a-kind cedar doors that once graced a house in northern Italy.

ABOVE Stripped of their original hardware, the doors were retrofitted with detailed antique bronze handles.

BELOW New glass backs up the wrought-iron and zinc grilles that are original to the doors. The handcrafted woodwork on the doors is highly detailed.

dress **u**p an **o**ld **d**oor

Does your front old door need TLC? That means a new paint job for starters. If the door has been painted many times, take it off its hinges and strip it before adding more layers of paint. You will have to strip it if you intend to display the original wood. If you can get away with just painting the door, sand it down first and use an exterior latex paint or a stain. Once you've got the door itself spruced up, you can fit it with new hardware, a knocker, or even new glass (below). Another way to restore a door is to replace the casing—the trim that conceals the gap between the door-jambs and the walls. You can opt for a built-up crosshead—a heavier, detailed horizontal molding that goes over the door and pilasters (right)—and simulated pillars that run along the sides of the door. Some molding manufacturers offer pieces that eliminate the need for any difficult miter cuts.

pathways and front stairs

There is something romantic about a meandering pathway with moss peeking from between the stones and garden flowers spilling over its edges. Contrasted with the hard-edged blacktop and sidewalks that lead us to places of work and commerce, garden paths offer the promise of a lovely surprise or much needed respite at the end. Integral parts of an entryway presentation are the pathway and steps that lead to the front door. It is fitting that the path leading to your house should evoke the promise of comfort and relaxation. If it doesn't in its current configuration, you might consider augmenting it or replacing it altogether.

To perform its proper function, a pathway should escort you and your guests from the most sensible place to park a car to the front door. If you park in a driveway and your guests park on the street, there should be two, possibly convergent, paths. Stairs, if necessary along the path or in front of the door, should have the standard dimensions for outdoor use: riser height of 5 to 6 inches and treads of at least 13 inches. Three or more steps call for a handrail. In terms of safety, pathways and stairs must be in good repair and constructed from material equal to the weather constraints where you live.

Typical pathway materials include brick, concrete pavers, poured concrete, natural stone, and tile. Stairs can be constructed of brick, concrete, wood, or a combination of any of these in addition to the choices for pathways. Building masonry stairs is usually the domain of a professional stone mason. A pathway can be successfully installed by a competent do-it-yourselfer, however. If the project is complex, a landscape designer can help you determine a new layout for your pathway or stairs and give you advice about what material will best complement the style and colors of your house.

If the existing pathway is basically sound, but visually lackluster, consider widening it with a contrasting paving material on either side. In some cases, you can even install a prettier path over an existing one. Adding plants that form an attractive border along the way can also improve its look. Lighting along a pathway and especially near steps is always a good idea.

OPPOSITE Cultivating greenery between paving stones gives a walkway color and interesting detail. You can add fragrance by planting an aromatic herb, too. Create interest by varying materials and textures.

ABOVE This pathway is narrow along the side of the house and widens in the front to distinguish the main entrance into the house.

LEFT Brick and stone have old-fashioned appeal. Here they are combined in the path and stairs leading up to the front door.

ABOVE Fieldstone risers and a stony stairway wall complement the stonework siding of this house. The masonry plays an important role in establishing the home's decorative theme, both indoors and out.

LEFT Iron handrails curve outward like arms outstretched for an embrace welcoming visitors into this home. Massing ferns along the front and back of the rails softens the hard edges of the stairs and makes a friendlier, finished presentation.

▌how to install a "crazy-pavement" walkway

1 Excavate the path to 4 in. deep. Stake hardboard strips along the edges as a form for the concrete. Install a grid of rebar, and pour the concrete to fill the trench.

2 When the concrete has set, remove the hardboard. Position stones that fit together well. Don't cement the stones until you have worked out a large section.

3 The pieces fit together like those of a jigsaw puzzle. However, you may need to cut a stone occasionally to make it fit. Use a circular saw with a diamond-tipped blade.

4 Lift the stones up one at a time. Put down a bed of mortar, smoothing over the empty spaces with a trowel. Firmly press a stone into the mortar, twisting it slightly.

5 Place a level over several stones, and pound the newly positioned stone in several spots with a rubber mallet until it is level with the others on all sides.

6 Stretch a string the length of a straight path, or run a hose along the curved sections of the walkway. Mark the edge of the pathway using a pencil.

7 Cut a clean edge following the pencil line using a circular saw fitted with a diamond-tipped blade. Be sure to wear a dust mask and protective eyewear.

8 Mix 1 part cement to 3 parts sand and water to make a thin batch of mortar. Apply the mixture using a grout bag. Remove excess mortar with a wet sponge and water.

LEFT Creating steps that extend well beyond either side of the threshold can expand the impact of an entryway. In this example, the stepped porch accommodates columns and a good-sized portico. The gray stone and slate present a handsome contrast to the asphalt driveway.

BELOW Generous concrete slabs and a carpet of green grass act as stairway treads and provide a safe toe-hold on this incline that leads from the street to the door.

RIGHT Pavers and bricks are an interesting combination that have been used here to enhance pattern and texture in the front walkway.

above all, stairs and walkways should be safe

underfoot ||||||

ABOVE LEFT Slate stairs will endure for many years. It's a material that works well with formal or traditional designs.
||
ABOVE Tile makes a beautiful paving choice, and it can be installed over concrete. Here it is used with an unusual contemporary dwelling.
||
LEFT In a country setting, a simple gravel path can be beautiful—especially when delineated by well-tended garden beds.

| fixing cracks and breaks

1 To make minor repairs of small cracks, start by cleaning out dirt and debris with a whisk broom.

2 Concrete repair caulk provides a quick fix for minor cracks. It prevents further damage but is only a temporary repair.

3 To patch larger areas and edges, clear out loose debris with a cold chisel. Add a form board to contain the patch.

4 Use masking tape to protect any adjacent surfaces where you don't want any fresh masonry to bond.

5 Apply a thin layer of bonding adhesive, which will help create a strong bond with the patch material.

6 Fill the damaged area with vinyl-reinforced patching compound in thin layers. Wait 30 min. between coats.

Brand-new windows can update the face of your house much in the same way a stylish pair of eyeglasses or a trendy hairstyle can give a person a lift. With today's new windows, tight seals and excellent insulation ratings are standard. There are shapes, sizes, and configurations to suit every whim. If your replacement windows are part of a larger exterior remodeling, your architect will assess your fenestration needs in terms of maximizing or controlling natural light, privacy, and style. If you decide to replace windows as a stand-alone project, you'll likely do this assessment yourself. So that you don't simply trade inadequate windows for other unsuitable ones, consider whether you want more or less natural light. Think carefully about style, as well. If you can't replace all of your windows at once, you might consider changing just those on the front of the house. Perhaps an accent window is enough to add pizzazz. Don't forget to give ample thought to what your windows reveal inside. When people look at windows, the view doesn't necessarily stop at the glass. Be sure to choose window treatments that are attractive and appropriate inside and out, too.

windows

LEFT As the casement windows of this turret demonstrate, there are specialty windows for just about any design specifications you can imagine.

OPPOSITE TOP LEFT An accent window can break up a boring expanse of wall or, in this case, a plain gable to provide an interesting focal point.

OPPOSITE TOP RIGHT The half-moon accent window makes the middle unit appear arched in imitation of a classical Palladian style.

OPPOSITE BOTTOM Windows added in conjunction with a complete house makeover can change the architecture.

add charm with window boxes and shutters

ABOVE LEFT You don't need new windows to have beautiful ones. With an easy-to-install trellis and lavish window boxes, this series of three enjoys a lovely frame of greenery.

ABOVE Window frames in natural wood is an option offered by some window manufacturers. Here, colorful flowers pop against the dark siding.

LEFT Shutters come in a variety of styles and shapes. These board-and-batten-style shutters, unlike their louvered or paneled counterparts, evoke informal, countrified style.

OPPOSITE TOP Window boxes filled with cascading blooms make short windows appear longer and in better proportion to the house size.

OPPOSITE BOTTOM Although they are strictly decorative, these board-and-batten shutters are arched to echo the shape of the windows they dress.

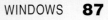

bright idea

shutter bugged

Installing exterior decorative shutters is an inexpensive way to add curb appeal. But if you live in an historic district, you may be mandated to use a certain type or style. Don't violate code; check with your building department.

For many people, a front porch calls to mind a time when life was slower, days seemed longer, and conversation was the best form of entertainment. Because of these warm, homey associations, a porch, in all its glory, can figure big when it comes to curb appeal. By the same token, one that's seen better days can detract from the appearance of a house. Sprucing up an older porch—whether it needs a complete overhaul or just some simple paint and redecorating—is a worthy endeavor. And thanks to the variety of stock millwork that's available today, it's fairly easy to achieve handsome results.

Front Porches

| popular porch styles |
| porch restoration |
| furnishing the porch |

A porch addition should blend with the style of the rest of the house. Rain-runoff control systems can be hidden by running downspouts behind or within columns.

The smallest "porch" is the front stoop. Sheltered by an eyebrow roof or a modest-sized bracketed canopy, the stoop offers just enough space to fumble with keys or shake off the rain, but little seating space. However, it does provide a transition, although slight, from outdoors to inside your home. If that's all you have, make the most of it

popular porch styles

with nice lighting, plants, and a chair, if there's room for one. Otherwise, think about adding a full-size porch to the front of your house. There are several classic architectural styles you might consider as a starting point for your design: gothic revival, Victorian gingerbread, and craftsman, to name a few. Houses of these eras often included *sitting porches*, which were specifically intended for outdoor relaxation and socializing during the summertime. Traditionally, the roof of a sitting porch is not an extension of the roofline of the house but a separate structure. It has balusters and rails or a wall connecting the roof supports that surround the porch. Modern-day versions can be screened, too. A *wraparound porch* is a sitting porch taken to its most extravagant form.

A *portico* is a small porch; *gallery* and *veranda* are popular Southern terms for a porch, which is especially useful there because it shields the interior of the house from the strong sun. The roof typically features a generous overhang that keeps the porch shady and cool. On the second floor, these shady spots are called *balconies.*

House styles intermingle, and so do porch styles, today. Which ones are right for you? Look here.

OPPOSITE TOP For many homeowners, a sprawling wraparound porch is the quintessential porch design. Lovingly restored along with the rest of this house, it invites outdoor living.

LEFT Sheltered by the roof overhangs, this modest front porch and balcony emphasize the pleasing symmetry of the architecture. Baluster styles on each level complement one another.

ABOVE A new columned porch features a cedar ceiling and recessed lighting. Its generous dimensions and formal style give the feeling of an outdoor foyer.

a front porch is like a friendly invitation

ABOVE Comfortably furnished, a spacious porch can function as a second living room—perfect for reading, entertaining, or drowsing in the summer air.

RIGHT A porch provides countless opportunities to include appealing touches to the entrance of your home. Here a large flower box adorns the porch rail with blooms.

OPPOSITE A porch that extends to either side of the entryway creates a lovely sheltered spot. Well-chosen furnishings that suit the scale of the space tie in with the overall color scheme and style of the house.

how **b**ig **s**hould **i**t **b**e?

Sketch possible plans, keeping in mind several things about size. Like any living space, a porch should be big enough to accommodate the activities you plan for it. It should also be in scale with the other elements of the house. Built too big or too small, a porch can be both ugly and dysfunctional.

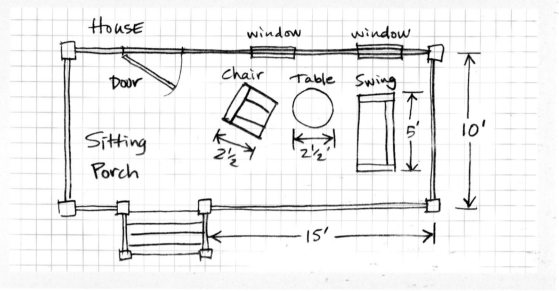

ABOVE Popular at the turn of the century, a balcony off the bedroom was once called a sleeping porch. This one is retrofitted with fancy latticework.

RIGHT This veranda features classical-styled columns, ornate trim, a gleaming beadboard ceiling, and a stone floor that's cool underfoot when shaded in summer.

OPPOSITE When a breathtaking view is part of the package, the porch configuration can conform to take advantage of it.

fresh air and sunshine

When thinking about location, consider how and when you plan to use the porch. An important consideration is its site orientation. Specifically, you need to know about the prevailing winds in your locale and how the sun will affect the porch space. Here are some general rules of thumb: a porch or sunroom with an eastern or northern exposure will be warmed by the sun in the mornings. Later in the day, the porch roof will block direct sunlight, so the space should be relatively pleasant in the afternoon and early evening, too. On the south or west side of your home, a porch or sunroom will be comfy in the morning but will cook in the afternoon and early evening sun. Awnings or some type of adjustable shading helps.

integrate a new porch into the existing house

bright idea

blue skies

Fair skies as far as the eye can see! The quaint practice of painting porch ceilings sky blue is enjoying a revival.

and your lifestyle

I t's likely that a vintage home, one built prior to the 1930s, originally featured a porch. If that porch still exists, there's a good possibility that it has sagged over the years.

The first step in restoring an old porch is to assess the posts, piers, or walls that support the deck. You want to ensure against sinking, expansion, and contraction. Check building codes.

Decking joists, generally made of wood, must be sized to accommodate the span and load of the deck. If they're not, update them. Repair or replace cracked concrete or rotting floorboards. The deck should slope away from the house slightly to allow rainwater runoff. Similarly, determine that the ledgers, where

porch restoration

the roof connects to the house; the ceiling joists; the ceiling planks; and the headers that secure joists to the columns or piers are all in good shape.

Once the porch is sound, it's time to think about style. An old porch may have had new balusters and rails added over the years—but perhaps not ones that conform to original architecture. If these elements are old, they may be wearing years of built-up paint. It's possible to get down to the wood by stripping off old paint, so repainting is an option. Should it prove too much of a job, new balusters, rails, and decorative trim options that keep with your home's style can go a long way toward bringing an old porch back to life.

OPPOSITE White wicker outfits this spacious porch for afternoon tea.

RIGHT TOP A cottage porch with climbing roses has a fairy-tale quality.

RIGHT CENTER Masonry piers hold up columns up that support the roof on this all-American front porch.

RIGHT BOTTOM Roller shades with natty stripes keep this space comfortable and private.

OPPOSITE TOP LEFT A hipped roof over the entry echoes this home's Dutch Colonial-style architecture. The arch mimics the shape of the half-round door transom.

ABOVE Here, Victorian corbels support a small sheltering roof.

OPPOSITE BOTTOM LEFT The steep pitch of the roof on this remodeled porch ties it into the rest of the house and, more importantly, draws attention to the entry.

OPPOSITE BOTTOM RIGHT Even a small covered landing can add extraordinary style. Here, a curved canopy relates beautifully to the graceful eliptical transom over the pair of entry doors and sidelights.

ABOVE RIGHT This pretty front porch extends the entry just enough for a couple of chairs.

pretty **p**ractical

When porches fell out of favor in the 1930s and 40s, new homeowners were often left in the rain while they fumbled for front-door keys. If your house has an exposed front door, consider adding a porch as a functional way to dress up the entry and provide extra outdoor living space. Appending an eyebrow roof or a small shed roof to the wall above the door can keep the rain off but does little to enhance the look of your home. A tastefully designed porch can keep you dry as you enter and exit the house. It can also accommodate a couple of chairs or a swing. Before proceeding, check with your local building department to find out about permits, codes, and regulations.

LEFT Classical columns raise the roof of this porch so that the top of the doorframe is clearly outlined, adding height and drama to the entryway.

RIGHT Millwork details are a staple of handsome porch design. This delicate sunburst set into the pediment continues the tradition.

OPPOSITE Shaped rafters and exposed roof sheathing give this porch ceiling a distinctive look.

incorporate elements that add style

ABOVE A custom lattice rail and framework offset this pocket porch and echo the cubed design created by the divided panes of the adjacent accent window.

LEFT Relatively easy-to-install corner brackets can reshape the framework between columns or beams. Use them to soften hard lines or draw your eye to other details.

Railing Styles

Rustic

- Handrail
- Trim
- Baluster
- Porch Post or Newel Post
- Trim
- Bottom Rail
- Porch Deck

Victorian

- Handrail
- Spacer fills groove in handrail between balusters.
- Baluster
- Porch Post or Newel Post
- Toenail baluster to rail.
- Bottom Rail
- Porch Deck

Classical

- Handrail
- Column
- Baluster
- Bottom Rail

ABOVE LEFT Incorporating elements such as an old chest of drawers and a sisal area rug draws some of the warmth of an indoor room to this open-air living space.

ABOVE RIGHT Don't skimp on style. This wrought-iron chair looks sophisticated in its setting, with plump cushions that have been covered in an all-weather fabric. Pottery provides the right amount of accessorizing.

OPPOSITE Rustic twig chairs with rattan seats, woven in a herringbone pattern, complement the natural stone elements of this veranda-style porch.

The outdoor-furnishings market abounds with a wide variety of items and styles. Depending on how sheltered your porch space is—and how extreme your climate—you may be able to bring small, traditional indoor furniture pieces outside for the summer. But not to worry, innovative materials and coatings now let you furnish outdoor living spaces comfortably without the concern of weather-related damage—and maintenance. That's good news because homeowners everywhere are enjoying outdoor living today. Look for treated fabrics and engineered materials that look like natural wood, stone, and metal. And always measure space before you buy. Think of arranging your porch the same way as you would arrange furniture inside your home. Leave space for conversation areas and easy passage. Stylewise, take your cues from the architecture but make it personal. Include unique items in your plan. If the porch

furnishing the porch

can accommodate it, put a rug underfoot. And don't forget lighting, including floor and table lamps or ceiling fans that have been designed especially for outdoor rooms. Search antique stores and flea markets for accessories and vintage outdoor pieces that add character.

bright idea

porch fans

For those lazy, hot summer days when nary a breath of wind stirs the soul or the air on the porch, consider installing a ceiling-mounted porch fan. Several manufacturers offer models built to endure the temperature extremes and humidity of an outdoor environment.

OPPOSITE Use the rafters for display. A collection of straw baskets suspended from above enhance the look of a country porch.

ABOVE LEFT Antique ironwork and urns have been used to compose an elegant focal point on this entry porch.

LEFT CENTER Use accessories to personalize the porch. Here, carved decoys usher visitors into the house.

LEFT Four all-weather wicker chairs and a small glass-top table create a stylish corner for alfresco dining.

ABOVE A screened porch can be a three-season room in many parts of the country.

M aking improvements to the driveway and garage, particularly if they can be seen from the street, will enhance your home's overall curb appeal, especially if you make sure these two features complement the style of your house and the surrounding property. Because they take up a lot of visual space, you'll have to find ways to keep them functional and attractive—but not distracting. As the following pages demonstrate, there are many stylish ways to improve the function and appearance of your driveway and garage without surrendering center stage to them.

Driveways and Garages

❙ driveway design ❙

❙ garages ❙

This spotless black asphalt driveway is neat but recedes from view, allowing the brick path to draw visitors to the entry. Simple garage doors blend with the house.

Driveway layouts may vary, but there are a few size and safety guidelines you should follow.

Plan the main part of the driveway to be between 10 to 12 feet wide for a one-car garage and 16 to 24 feet wide for a two-car garage. (If the driveway will form part of a walkway, add another 2 feet.) While a narrow driveway (6 to 8 feet wide) may suffice, it's better to make it wider so that people can step out onto the pavement and not onto grass or flower beds. An apron that tapers outward to meet the street makes it easier to back your car in or out. Extra parking that doesn't obstruct normal activities is useful; allow 12 feet per vehicle for cars, more for trucks and RVs. You can screen these areas with plantings or fences. For safety's sake, don't crowd the walkway from the parking area to the entry door with plantings or other obstructions. Keep this area fully visible to maximize security.

A concrete driveway need be only 4 inches thick for normal car traffic. However, if you expect heavy trucks, you should increase the thickness to at least 6 inches. Because a variety of vehicles might use the end of the driveway to turn around, make that part at least 8 inches thick. Keep in mind that proper drainage is critical. Any water that collects on the driveway will produce ice in the winter and will puddle near your house during heavy rains.

driveway design

OPPOSITE A driveway made of compressed earth underlies the simplicity and freedom from structure that is part of an informal country setting.

ABOVE RIGHT This asphalt driveway is wide enough to accommodate a spacious two-car garage.

RIGHT Crushed stones were used to create a curving driveway for this seaside house.

material **o**ptions

▌ **Brick, flagstone, and cobblestone** are distinctive driveway choices. They are usually installed over a bed of gravel and sand in a particular pattern. The materials are costly relative to other paving materials, and installation is time consuming. All are durable and require occasional washing, sealing, and weed control.

▌ **Interlocking pavers** are manufactured stone products that fit together to form a stable surface in an attractive pattern. Pavers come in a wide array of styles, colors, and prices. Installation, durability, and maintenance are similar to that of brick or cobblestone. Some pavers come with a warranty.

▌ **Concrete** is the most versatile choice. It can be colored and shaped; stamped with patterns that simulate stone, marble, tile, brick, or cobbles; embedded with stone or aggregates; or molded to create pavers. Concrete is generally inexpensive, but it can become more expensive if decorated or treated.

▌ **Asphalt** is inexpensive by comparison with most other materials, and durable. It requires a sealer coat every 2 to 3 years and periodic washing.

▌ **Stone gravel** is the most economical choice. Yearly restoning and weed control are necessary to maintain a good-looking stone driveway.

ABOVE Interlocking pavers with a decorative medallion woven into the design resemble bricks.

▌

OPPOSITE TOP LEFT A generous circular driveway comprising old brick answers the call for Old World elegance as demanded by this stately home.

▌

OPPOSITE TOP RIGHT A concrete grid with slate accents adds style to a large driveway in front of the entry.

▌

OPPOSITE BOTTOM Crushed stone, or gravel, can be a good-looking yet affordable paving option, especially if the driveway is large. But if you live in snow country, be warned: plowing causes a mess.

ABOVE LEFT While brick laid in the same pattern as that on the house would have appeared monotonous, the herringbone pattern on this driveway provides just the right amount of contrast.

LEFT A long gravel drive leads to a parking area and garage situated on the side of this house. If the option exists, locate parking away from the front of the house.

ABOVE RIGHT Keep it simple; don't let the driveway dominate the front of the property.

RIGHT A circular drive combines elegance with convenience.

design **o**ptions

Safety is the most important thing to consider when designing your driveway. If your house is on a busy street, take extra yard space for a turnaround so you don't have to back out. The figures given in these diagrams should be considered minimums; always consult with your building inspector before beginning work because local codes may be different.

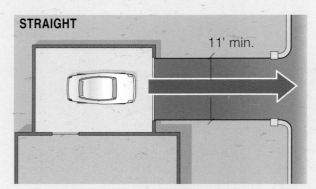

STRAIGHT

11' min.

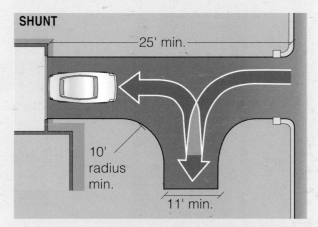

SHUNT

25' min.

10' radius min.

11' min.

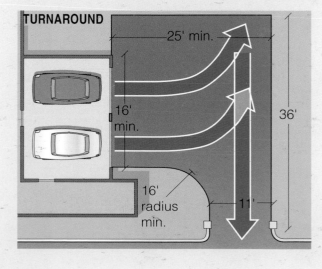

TURNAROUND

25' min.

16' min.

36'

16' radius min.

11'

color, pattern, and texture drive today's designs

bright idea

heated driveways

Installing a new driveway? Consider including a snow-melt system. Using heated water pumped through tubes installed under the driveway, it can put an end to shoveling and ice.

LEFT Tan-colored stones look great with the home's siding, stone foundation, and retaining wall.

OPPOSITE BOTTOM The most versatile driveway option, concrete, can be colored, patterned, shaped, or embedded with stone to give the appearance of a more textured surface. Here, a series of red-toned concrete pavers with gray accents create the illusion of brick.

RIGHT Combining materials adds more interest to a mundane surface such as asphalt. Bricks outline a curving driveway here.

BELOW Crushed gray stones coordinate beautifully with the color of the roof and the siding on this house. They also add texture to make a large driveway visually more sophisticated.

slope and drainage

If there is no natural slope to your driveway, it must be shaped to allow for drainage. Three possibilities illustrated at right include the crown (top), concave (middle), and cross-slope (bottom). Below: the ramp can have a slope of anywhere from 4–8%; the steeper the ramp, the gentler the slope of the apron. Ramps with 6–8% slopes should have aprons with 2% slopes or less.

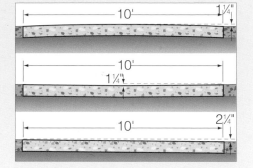

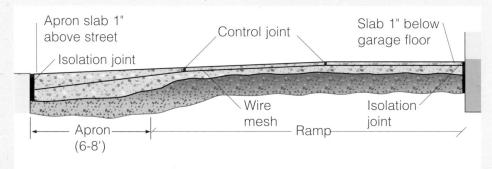

BELOW LEFT A carport on the side of the house looks elegant and blends seamlessly with the architecture.

BELOW This automatic wooden gate is understated and refined—and blocks the view of a long, unimpressive driveway.

OPPOSITE TOP Because the garage is located at the back of the property, an attached carport shelters quick and easy access to this house.

OPPOSITE BOTTOM A wide driveway gate becomes an important design feature with abstract metalwork applied to the front.

garages

How easy it will be to assimilate your garage into your overall curb-appeal plans largely depends on where it is situated on your property. The garage is the vestigial carriage house of bygone times. Older houses tend to include a garage that is unattached and off to the side or set back from the main house. But that option became trickier for architects to accommodate as building lots shrunk and demands for lower-cost housing grew. Hence many modern homeowners now live with attached garages that can detract from the front of the house, especially as garages have become bigger to meet the needs of the multi-vehicle family. The location is great for convenience, but it creates an aesthetic challenge. Fortunately, garage doors finally come in many styles to complement any house. In fact, they can actually boost overall architectural appeal in many cases. While the main focus of an attached garage could be the style of the door, the size of the structure itself, whether or not it's attached, should be in proportion to the house and in keeping with the architecture. To create a unified image, coordinate the siding and roofing materials and the color used on the body of the structures and the trim. And don't forget: attractive lighting and landscaping are just as important to the garage as they are to your house.

garage door options

The most durable and best performing material options for garage doors are *wood* and *steel*. Wood doors are more traditional and allow for complete customization of color. They are sturdy and excellent insulators, even when not reinforced with insulation. Steel doors are heavier, sturdier, and generally a bit less costly than wood. Both come with the option for insulation. In either case, insulation is sandwiched between the outer door and an inner face. There are two kinds of insulation—polystyrene foam and injected foam. The injected foam provides a slightly better insulating value than does polystyrene. An insulated door is a good option if you use the space for any kind of activity or if you store items that require protection from extreme temperatures. It is also a good idea if the garage forms a barrier between living space and the outside.

Two other material options for garage doors are *aluminum* and *fiberglass*. While they are sometimes economical, they will not stand up to much abuse and are more difficult to keep looking good.

Garage doors come in *single-panel* or *sectional* roll-up styles. The single-panel door tilts up and projects out before it glides out of sight above the opening. The garage-door opening must be cleared of snow or anything else for the door to operate. The car must be a certain distance back from the door. The sectional style rolls straight up into a track and out of sight above the opening. The car can be pulled right up to the door, and the door can still operate. If you've opted for a sectional roll-up door, you have another choice to make between extension or torsion springs. Traditional garage doors and all single-panel doors operate with extension springs that expand and contract when you open and close the doors. Torsion springs feature a shaft spring and drum assembly that cannot break and distributes the door's weight more evenly. It costs more but is safer.

A wood door is generally unfinished and requires staining or painting both initially and then periodically for maintenance. A steel door will have a durable ready finish. The only maintenance required is cleaning. If you want to change the finish of your door occasionally, wood is a better choice.

When it comes to appearances, you can find nearly any door style imaginable in a garage door. Traditional raised-panel doors with glazing of regular or decorator glass are widely available. Raised panels in contrasting colors to the door frame are another smart-looking option. Most manufacturers offer doors to complement particular architectural styles, too. Styles that simulate doors that open out, whether it be a barn door look-alike or a carriage-house door imitator, can lend an element of elegance. For more contemporary settings, you can opt for doors that feature a stainless-steel finish or steel and glass.

When shopping for a garage door, check out home stores or the Internet. Online, you can visit manufacturers' web sites to see their stock doors, as well as semi-customizable lines. Predictably, the more styling the door features, the more you can expect to pay. The price differential between a basic stock door and its semi-custom or custom counterpart can be as much as $2,500.

ABOVE Steel doors with frosted-glass panels resemble Japanese Shoji screens and coordinate with the home's Asian-influenced architecture. Accent lighting heightens the impact.

BELOW Raised-panel doors, hardware, and a lighting fixture that matches the colonial look of the house adds style to this two-car garage.

OPPOSITE TOP "Divided lights" echo the muntined windows on the house.

OPPOSITE BOTTOM These new custom-made garage doors have been crafted in wood to resemble authentic carriage-house doors.

OPPOSITE Wood doors, old or new, offer the advantage of versatility. You can always strip them down and repaint them to coordinate with whatever colors you choose for the rest of your house. If the doors are old, reglazing the glass is another option that can add new life. These creamy yellow doors offer just enough color to accent but not overwhelm the neutral stain on the siding.

OPPOSITE BOTTOM Shed dormers keep this super-sized garage from looking like an uninteresting block building. The siding and roofing were selected to match the materials on the house.

BELOW A bit of gingerbread trim adds a charming note to a vintage structure that has been well maintained over the years. Because the garage is on the side of the house, fresh paint is all that's necessary to keep these doors looking good.

installing new doors

Installing a new overhead door can give a boost to your home's appearance. (See before and after photos, below.) The project is trickier than installing most other kinds of doors, but it's not beyond most do-it-yourselfers. The key is to identify and organize the dozens of parts and follow the manufacturer's instructions. You'll need a drill and a socket wrench set in addition to a level, measuring tape, and some other basic carpentry tools.

Overhead doors are typically trouble-free, provided you keep the hardware tight, clean, and lubricated. It's also important to maintain the exterior finish, particularly on raised-panel-style wood doors, which are subject to rot. Check them annually for cracks in the paint, and caulk seals along the joints.

BEFORE

AFTER

Nothing can spoil the exterior appearance of a house as much as a neglected front yard. Talk about a poor first impression! Maintaining a healthy lawn and regularly tending garden beds and other plantings are important to keeping your home's curb-appeal quotient high. Even better, a thoughtful landscape plan will work with your home's architecture and provide color, pattern, and texture to complement your house year-round. Good landscape design also helps with practical matters, such as delineating space, buffering noise, camouflaging unwelcome views, and ensuring privacy.

Landscape Appeal

❚ rejuvenate the front lawn ❚ proper mowing and watering ❚ personal style ❚ trees and shrubs ❚ hardscaping ❚ ❚ six designs ❚

Landscaping is the one type of design that changes over time as plants grow and adapt with the season. Combine plants with hardscapes to create eye-catching curb appeal.

rejuvenate the front lawn

In some home landscapes, the front lawn is there by default to cover bare ground rather than as a deliberate part of a general plan. Sometimes, it's the only dominant landscape feature visible from the street. Unfortunately, some homeowners do not realize that a lawn is simply one possibility in an overall design that may feature a variety of natural elements that work with the natural conditions of the site, the soil, and the climate of a location. In fact, a traditional lawn may not be part of your landscape plan at all. But if it is, make the most of it, by cultivating an emerald carpet, which you can surround with flowers, shrubs, and trees. The ideal lawn grass is fine-textured and a deep, rich green. It should grow in a dense mat to keep out weeds. However, there is no one all-purpose grass that does well everywhere and meets all kinds of needs. Research or consult a landscape specialist in your area to find out which of the more than 40 kinds of grass will thrive for you.

OPPOSITE To create a varied front-yard landscape, treat the lawn as one of many elements in the design.

LEFT Sometimes the best approach is to remove the lawn entirely and replace it with ground cover as in this landscape.

ABOVE Large front lawns help create a park-like setting. Be sure to add shrubs and trees to create vertical interest.

today's grass has been bred for lasting performance

ABOVE Often the size of the lawn will depend on the size of the front yard. In the case of the landscape above, the lawn serves as a kind of canvas for the plantings, fences, and other elements located close to the house.

LEFT A manicured and well-tended lawn, low-growing shrubs in the front, and tall trees to the side frame this distinctive-looking house, enhancing rather than competing with its architectural details.

▌ how to sow seed

In addition to being less expensive than sod or even plugs and sprigs, seed provides a better choice of new high-quality cultivars. You can choose the grass type that will do best in your specific garden. However, there are a few drawbacks to sowing seed. It takes about a month for a newly seeded lawn to fill in, and several months for it to be durable enough for heavy use. In the meantime, there is a risk that the seed will wash away or be eaten by birds and that weeds will grow along with the grass.

Warm-season grasses germinate best when the soil is warm, between 70° and 90°F. To ensure a speedy and high rate of germination, wait to sow grass seed until late spring or early summer. Don't wait too long, however, or you'll risk giving the newly sown grass too short a growing season.

Late summer or early autumn, when the weather is cooling, is ideal for sowing (or overseeding) cool-season lawns. Cooler temperatures stimulate the germination process, and the autumn rains will relieve you of some of the watering chores. In northern climates, some people overseed their cool-season lawns in spring to fill in bare or thin patches and to improve the overall vigor of the lawn. Although possible, success is harder to achieve at that time of year. You must water faithfully until the grass is well-rooted and hope that the weather stays cool long enough so that the summer heat doesn't damage young, tender roots.

Scatter the grass seed evenly over the soil. You can use a spreader, but if you prefer to scatter the grass seed by hand, walk in one direction first, then walk perpendicular across the lawn to ensure full coverage. If you use a spreader, set it to release the grass seed at the rate recommended on the seed package label.

Once you have spread the seed, rake lightly over the surface to scratch it into the soil, but don't bury it too deeply. All you really want to do is make good contact between the seed and the soil. Then lightly spread organic mulch, such as compost or straw, over the area to help keep the seed moist.

Use a fine water spray to thoroughly moisten both grass seed and ground. Grass seed must continually be kept moist until it has germinated. If the weather is hot and dry the first week, you may need to water as frequently as three times a day. Once the roots start growing, you can back off to daily watering until the lawn looks strong. Rope off the seeded area to discourage people and animals from walking across. If seed-eating birds are a problem, try tying strips of torn sheets or rags on the rope at regular intervals. They'll frighten the birds when they flap in the breeze.

Don't mow a newly seeded lawn for at least four to six weeks. If you do, you may tear up the shallow-rooted grass plants.

1 **Spread the Seed.** Aim for coverage of between 15 to 20 seeds per square inch after you've crossed the lawn twice with the spreader.

2 **Rake the Seeded Surface.** Rake lightly to mix the seed into the top ⅛ inch of soil. The raking can also disperse seed that was spread too thickly.

3 **Nurture the Young Plants.** Keep newly sprouted grass moist, watering twice a day if there is no rain. Maintain this level of moisture until the plants are 2 inches tall.

| how to fix a bare patch

Lawns occasionally develop bare patches, which should be repaired so that they don't detract from the look of the rest of the lawn. Bare spots can be fixed easily by over-seeding, a process similar to seeding, except in a smaller area. If you live in the northern part of the United States, the best time to overseed is in late summer and early fall. If you live in the Southern states, the recommended time is spring or early summer. Before you begin, choose an appropriate seed, so that your patch will blend with the rest of the lawn when it has grown in. Roughen the surface with a garden pitchfork or rake before you scatter any seed. Then spread the seed with your hand or a spreader.

1 **Loosen the Soil.** To repair a bare patch of lawn, use a pitchfork to loosen the soil in the bare spot to a depth of 6 to 8 inches.

2 **Level the Soil**. Drag the flat end of a landscape rake over the patch to level the planting surface and remove all debris.

3 **Spread the Seed.** With your hand, evenly spread a mixture of seed, fertilizer, and soil over the affected area.

4 **Tamp the Seeds Down.** Use the flat end of the rake to tamp the seeds into the soil, or roll with a one-third full roller.

bright idea

Kid proof

Plant a sturdy grass, such as perennial rye or Bermudagrass, if your kids play on the grass.

LEFT Don't forget the views of the side of your house, especially if you live on a corner lot. Here the small area of lawn serves as a backdrop for the brightly colored flowers.

BELOW If the lawn will be used by children as a play space, choose a tough variety of grass and protect border plants using low walls or fences.

ABOVE Break up a large expanse of lawn by planting trees and shrubs. Create even more interest by surrounding tall elements with ground cover.

BELOW Use the lawn as a pathway between garden elements, such as a bridge between two borders or flower beds or between a patio and a planting area. Here the lawn connects a planting area with the front of the house.

how to lay sod

Sod is strips of growing lawn that have been cut out of the ground. Although more expensive than sowing a lawn from seed or plugs, sod provides instant coverage. When you order sod, have it delivered when it can be laid immediately. Even a few hours in the sun can damage the grass.

First, moisten the ground where you plan to put the sod. Then lay the sod, butting ends of adjoining strips together but not overlapping them. Work from the sodded area to the

1 Cut the Sod into Pieces. Use a sharp trowel to cut sod to fit at butt joints (shown above) or when cutting against a straightedge. You may also use the trowel to level any irregularities in the soil.

4 Cut the Last Piece to Fit. After you have laid sod to the opposite side of the area in which you're working, cut the next-to-last piece to fit. Before cutting, roll out the sod for a test fit.

open soil. To protect the already laid sod from excess foot traffic, place a plywood sheet over the surface while you are working.

Tamp down the soil to ensure that the roots make good contact with the soil, and then water thoroughly. The traditional way to tamp sod is to roll a water-filled roller over it.

Water within 30 minutes of laying the sod. Irrigate daily for the first 10 days; then back off to every second or third day until the new roots are well developed. It should take from two to four weeks for the sod to become properly established. After that, water slowly and deeply so that the water penetrates at least 6 inches into the soil. This method will encourage a deep root system that is more drought-tolerant than shallow-rooted grass. The average lawn needs about 1 inch of water on a weekly basis. Depending on the type of soil (heavy clay versus sandy, for example), it may take anywhere from 10 minutes to several hours for an inch of water to penetrate.

2 **Lay the Sod.** It's important to have full strips at the perimeter; narrow strips dry out faster than wide ones. As you lay the sod, keep all joints as tight as possible, but avoid overlapping or stretching the sod.

3 **Fit Sections Together.** When fitting two pieces of sod at an odd angle, lay one piece over the other, and cut through both at once. Then lift the top piece, and remove the waste underneath.

5 **Roll the New Sod Lawn.** If necessary, use an edger to trim between the edge of the sod and the bed. Then use a water-filled roller to eliminate air pockets and ensure that the roots make good contact with the soil.

6 **Clean Up Any Remaining Soil.** Fill the joints between strips with fine soil. Use a small, flexible rake to work any excess soil into the cracks between pieces of sod. Always stand on the board to protect planted areas.

proper mowing and

best mowing heights

Grass Type	Finished Height
Bluegrass	2 inches
Perennial ryegrass	2 inches
Tall fescue	2 inches
Fine fescue	2 inches
St. Augustinegrass	2 inches
Buffalograss	2 inches
Bermudagrass	1½ inches
Zoysiagrass	1½ inches
Centipedegrass	1½ inches

Source: The Lawn Institute (Marietta, Georgia)

ABOVE Lawn care is about more than watering and fertilizing. Be sure to mow to the height that is best for your variety of grass.

OPPOSITE Water deeply to encourage grass roots to grow downward, strengthening the leaves. Base the amount of water you provide on the type of soil in your yard.

Many lawn problems are a result of cutting grass too short. Grass that is shorn too close is more likely to succumb to stresses caused by drought, insect injury, foot traffic, or inadequate sun. Ideally you should never remove more than one-third of the leaf surface each time you mow. See the table on the opposite page for guidelines on ideal heights for different grasses. The lawn's rate of growth—and therefore how often you need to mow—will depend on how warm the weather is, how much water the lawn has received, and whether you fertilized. Those factors will vary throughout the season, although most people find that a schedule of weekly mowing works well.

At least once a year you should sharpen your lawn mower blades. Blunt mower blades can ruin a lawn by tearing the leaves. Each torn blade will die back ⅛ to ¼ inch, giving the lawn a brown tinge. The ragged edge makes the grass susceptible to disease.

Lawns grow best when they are watered deeply and infrequently. The deep water penetration encourages roots to grow down, rather than sideways, improving the root structure and drought tolerance of the grass. If your soil is dense clay, water slowly so that the water can soak in rather than run off. The

watering

average lawn needs about 1 inch of water on a weekly basis. If your soil is a heavy clay, it can take as long as 5 hours for 1 inch of water to penetrate properly. At the other extreme, sandy soil will absorb 1 inch of water in approximately 10 minutes. To determine how much water you are delivering, space shallow cans at regular intervals along your lawn and time how long it takes them to fill. One inch of water will penetrate about 12 inches in sandy soil, 7 inches in loam, and 4 to 5 inches in clay. If you have clay soil and want to water the lawn to a depth of 6 inches, you would need to leave the sprinkler on until there is 1½ inches of water in each container. Water to a depth of 6 to 12 inches.

Water lawns early in the morning or late in the afternoon. It is generally less windy at those times of day, so you cut down on wind-blown losses. Also, the cooler temperatures will minimize evaporation.

when to fertilize

The best time to fertilize a lawn is when it is actively growing.

❙ Cool-season grasses grow best in spring and fall, so fertilize cool-season grasses at the beginning of the growing season in spring or as cooler temperatures return in fall.

❙ If you plan to fertilize at regular intervals over a period of months in spring, stop as soon as the weather gets hotter. If you like, you can feed once more in autumn after the first frost to set up the lawn for next spring's growth.

❙ Feed warm-season grasses in late spring and again in August.

❙ If you are using a slow-release form of nitrogen, feed smaller doses every six to ten weeks until about eight weeks before the first frost date.

❙ If the lawn has good color and is growing well, delay additional feedings by a week or two.

❙ Overfeeding a lawn is wasteful and damaging to the environment. Excess fertilizer may be leached out by watering and carried into underground water systems.

LEFT Think color and texture when selecting plants and structures to include in your home landscape.

BELOW You have many options. Create designs that show off your personal style.

OPPOSITE Take landscaping cues from the sur-roundings and from the materials used on the house. Note the organic look of the house and plantings shown here.

Today's homeowners have access to an amazing palette of plants, and new-and-improved hybrids are introduced yearly. The fun—and challenge—is combining plants that serve specific design functions, look beautiful together, and grow well in your region. You can then arrange the plants, often called softscaping, with hardscaping elements, such as stones, paths, patios, and walls, to create an environment that pleases you. In this process, you'll begin expressing your own vision of paradise—a place of bliss, felicity, and delight. You can copy one of the established styles or develop your own. (See the sample landscape designs that are illustrated on pages 158-163.) The

personal style

landscaping of many new suburban front gardens usually features shrubs or plantings that hug the foundation, a walkway leading from the driveway to the front door, and a sapling that may one day become a tree. Sometimes, the front lawn also features an island bed with shrubs and ground covers. Typically, in the backyard, there's a patio or deck and a lawn surrounded with perimeter beds of shrubs, one or two perennials, and maybe some roses. But what you might see in your neighborhood does not necessarily need to apply to your lifestyle. Try rethinking the front yard.

There are many design options from which to choose. For example, instead of leaving the front of the house exposed to the street with just a lawn as a transition, consider creating a private garden room that serves as an outdoor foyer. You can do this by planting shrubs around the edge of the front of your property instead of cramming them up against the house foundation. Design the area so that the path leading from the driveway or street directs traffic to the garden room. Enlarge this area so that it is wider than the path. Add a bench, and plant tall shrubs for privacy. Use trellises or arbors for more interest.

look at your front yard with a fresh eye

create a landscape base map

You can create a base map from a copy of your plat (or property survey) prepared by surveyors, which most homeowners receive when they purchase their house. A plat typically shows several individual properties and may or may not show structures, including houses. If you don't have a plat, request one from your tax assessor's office; copies are usually available at no cost or for a nominal fee.

In addition to showing locations of property lines, a footprint of the house, and any other significant structures, the plat should show easements and the location of overhead and underground utility lines owned by the county or city. It should also have a legend indicating its drawing scale, which is typically 1:20, meaning that every inch on the paper is equivalent to 20 feet on your property. If the scale isn't shown, you can calculate it by measuring a distance on the plat in inches and then correlating that with the same actual distance on your property.

Make several enlarged copies. Property surveys and plats are usually a standard size, which is tiny considering all the information you want to record. Take your plat or property survey to a copy shop or blueprint company to get an enlargement. While you're there, you might as well have them make four or five copies, one for your site analysis, one for drawing your design, and extras for updates and changes over the years. If you can, have the blueprint company enlarge the original scale to at least 1:12. This will give you more room to draw garden features.

Even if your map shows the primary dimensions of your property, you'll need to take other measurements. This task will be easier if you use a fiberglass, nylon-clad steel, or chrome-steel measuring tape on a reel. These tapes, which are noted here in order from the least- to most-expensive type, come in longer lengths than the retractable version and are more suited to measuring larger spaces.

ABOVE Creating multiple levels that lead up to the front entry adds dramatic visual interest. Using a combination of stone steps, curving paths, and a variety of plant types, the designer created a distinctive entry area that is pleasing to both passersby and people walking up to the front door.

RIGHT The concept of outdoor rooms is becoming more and more popular. Here a shaded patio area is a link to the front door, but it is also a place where visitors can linger before approaching the door.

Typical
Plat Map

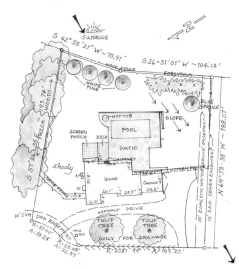

A plat map shows the precise boundaries, the measurements of the lot, and the position of the house, garage, and existing easements. Get one from the tax assessor's office.

Completing a base map is an important first step in landscaping. Here the owner has indicated extensive information about his property and plans.

summer sun

The sun and shade patterns change over the course of the year. In the winter, when the sun is low in the sky, the shadows cast by the deciduous tree and shrubs are longer than those cast in the summer sun (above). Take the sun's pattern into consideration when you choose other plants.

play up great features

"Accentuate the positive, eliminate the negative." So goes an old song by Johnny Mercer and Harold Arlen. The same philosophy applies to landscaping. Try to showcase the positive features of your property, such as a beautiful view, established trees and shrubs, large windows in your home that look onto the garden, or cooling summer breezes. Work to create a landscape design that emphasizes and enhances these good features.

If your land is evenly rectangular, you may want to make it appear more interesting by breaking up the space so that the entire back or front garden can't be seen at once. A screen of plants, a trellis, or a wall can divide a property, creating separate garden rooms.

An unevenly dimensioned lot offers both a challenge and an opportunity. For example, on a triangular lot, you can partition the narrow end from the rest of the lot by means of a hedge or fence. Include a narrow gate or doorway to give access to a secret retreat.

You can draw attention to a pretty view by framing it with a pair of trees, an arbor, or a pair of statues. Preserve panoramic views by keeping the plantings low so that the vista isn't obscured. If a distant view is just visible through a gap in the trees or between two buildings, use paths or other landscape elements to draw attention to the distant scene. Above all, if you have a good view, create a comfortable place where you can sit and enjoy it.

ABOVE An awkward triangle-shaped lot is divided into two garden rooms, transforming a challenging space into an asset. The front garden has more usefully proportioned shape, and the hidden, pointed garden beyond is a gem.

LEFT Consider scale when selecting features and plants for your landscape. Two-story houses like this one usually look best with tall trees; one-story houses look best with shorter trees and shrubs.

BELOW LEFT Notice how the low fence in this garden provides a sense of enclosure without overpowering the plants.

BELOW Paths are important landscape design elements. The width of the path, the materials you select, lighting, and the plants around it all contribute to the path's impact.

bright idea

logical course

Although you want your property to be aesthetically pleasing, it should also be convenient to use. Keep human needs in mind. For example, make sure a path follows a route that members of the household normally walk.

trees and shrubs

In old, established yards, you may need to remove or rejuvenate overgrown trees and shrubs to reclaim the original structure of the landscape's design. If you are starting from scratch, you should plan the trees and shrubs that will define the structure of the landscape before you begin thinking of details such as ground covers or flowers. Choose trees and shrubs that will help define spaces, provide focal points, or serve as a background foil to other plantings.

Don't overlook the importance of key plants with a bold or unusual shape. A tree or shrub that naturally grows in a striking form, such as a dogwood, or a spectacular specimen tree, such as a monumental chestnut or beech tree, makes a fascinating focal point, giving structure and visual direction to the overall design. If your property already has a significant, established tree, try to design your landscape to emphasize that asset.

Trees and shrubs have the potential to be the greatest asset in your garden, or the greatest liability if you do not choose the right ones.

If you want to plant a tree or shrub as a focal point in the center of a lawn, you can choose a large spreading specimen that will become ever more spectacular as it grows. But if you want to plant a tree along a driveway or patio, don't choose one with invasive roots. For example, weeping willow roots search insistently for water, even boring through pipes, and can heave up a concrete walkway or crack a house foundation. Stay away from messy trees that shed regularly or drop sticky fruit or sap, creating the need for frequent cleanup.

OPPOSITE Plants flank masonry steps that lead to a gated pathway. Each grouping contains low-growing shrubs that surround a taller specimen.

TOP Shrubs planted along a walkway help define the path. In cases such as this, it is best to keep the shrubs pruned to prevent them from blocking the path.

LEFT Place trees and shrubs where they won't block the view. Here a tall tree enhances the corner of the porch without obscuring the rest of the house.

selecting **t**rees

Before you buy a tree, draw a plan for your landscape that considers design, along with appropriate species and their placement. Investigate every characteristic of a tree you are considering using. Consider placement in relation to the house. (Site large trees at least 20 feet away from foundations, small ones at least 8 feet away). Many trees, even small ones, are planted too close to buildings; they eventually outgrow the space, make the building hard to maintain, and can reduce air circulation enough to promote structural rot in your house.

One-Story Considerations

Poor   Better

Two-Story Considerations

Poor   Better

One-story houses usually appear in better scale with small to midsize trees. At top left, the tall trees dwarf the house. And the tall conifer visually divides the house in half, while blocking the view from inside year-round. Taller houses tend to look better with at least a few taller trees. The short trees at bottom left make this house tower. The trees at right (top and bottom) appear more in scale with the house and lend an informal balance. Low shrubs near the house won't ever block the view from inside.

selecting shrubs

Shrubs, because of their smaller size and bushy shape, have a vital role in the garden, serving as the framework that connects the verticals of the trees and the horizontal lines of ground covers and flower borders and offering an immense variety of form, color, and texture. Enduring from year to year, shrubs provide interest in all seasons and usually need little maintenance. In a traditional herbaceous border, shrubs are the permanent backdrop for showy annuals and perennials. But a simple combination of shrubs and ground covers can be attractive and requires minimal upkeep.

Columnar   Arching   Pyramidal   Rounded   Sprawling or Prostrate

OPPOSITE Shrubs serve as foundation plantings. They also help define the informal stepping-stone path.

LEFT Flowering hydrangeas bloom almost all summer. Here they blend in a bed that also contains lavender.

BELOW Large shrubs appear to guard a front entry. Keep shrubs and trees in scale with the rest of the house.

hardscaping

Landscape designs often benefit from vertical elements such as walls, fences, arches, arbors, pergolas, and decorative freestanding plant supports. Walls and fences help define boundaries while enclosing special spaces. Properly positioned, an arbor or arch is an eye-catching accent, adding visual drama to the scene and providing an attractive focal point or point of passage between two parts of the garden. A pergola transforms an ordinary path into a special, shaded, and sheltered passageway, while a freestanding plant support is like an exclamation point, drawing attention to itself and creating a pleasant focus.

As an added bonus, any one of these features provides an opportunity to grow and enjoy the wide range of climbing plants such as clematis, wisteria, climbing roses, honeysuckle, trumpet vine, and jasmine. These vertical plants add a sense of lushness to the garden as they scramble up walls and over trellised arches or droop heavy panicles of flowers through the open fretwork ceiling of a pergola. Here are some ideas for hardscaping your front yard with these elements.

LEFT Fences not only serve as boundary markers, they are a design element in their own right. There are so many styles from which to choose that you should have no trouble finding one that is both functional and decorative. The posts on this classic style are topped with decorative finials.

RIGHT The brick wall that encloses this garden complements the brick pathway. Both have weathered to the point where they look as though they have always been part of the setting.

BELOW Consider installing a fence as a backdrop to a group of lush plantings. This simple rail fence defines the garden path and separates the front yard from the side yard, but it also seems to support the flowering plants.

BELOW The classic picket fence can be used with a variety of house styles. A purely decorative section of fence spans an opening in a hedge that borders the front yard of this house.

RIGHT A traditional picket fence serves as a backdrop for a group of border plants. In addition to their utilitarian functions, vertical elements such as fences and walls add texture and visual interest to a landscape.

BELOW RIGHT Fence posts, especially posts that mark an entry, can become focal points if you add special cap treatments or adorn one with fresh flowers.

designing a fence

Erecting a fence is the quickest and generally easiest way to define the boundary of your property. To be a successful part of a landscape design, a fence should be planned to complement the architecture of your house, possibly even echoing a distinctive design feature. Also bear in mind the character of your neighborhood and region. Your fence may be beautiful in and of itself but look out of place in the neighborhood where you live. In addition to style, other considerations for making a fence harmonious with its surroundings include height, color, and material.

With that in mind, the possibilities for fence designs are limitless. Traditional options include wrought iron, wooden pickets (or palings), stockade, split-rail, double- and triple-bar ranch fences, and even chain-link fences. Within those basic styles are many variations. For example, iron can be wrought in fanciful designs from modern clean-cut to the fancy curlicues of the Romanesque style. Picket points can take the form of arrows, fleurs-de-lis, or any other design. The pickets can be spaced in a variety of ways. Stockade fences can be closed- or open-board, or have angled paling boards. To add extra charm and interest, a solid wooden fence can be topped with lattice.

FENCE ANATOMY

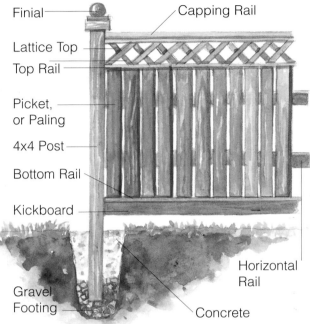

Finial

Capping Rail

Lattice Top

Top Rail

Picket, or Paling

4x4 Post

Bottom Rail

Kickboard

Horizontal Rail

Gravel Footing

Concrete

The main components of a board fence are pickets, horizontal rails, a top rail to protect the end grain of the pickets from moisture, the kickboard, and the support post.

BUILDING FENCES ON SLOPES

A slope presents a special challenge for fence design as fence sections are generally straight and parallel with the ground. Three possible solutions include stepping the fence down the slope, allowing gaps to occur as the slope progresses downward; building the fence to follow the hillside so that the top of the fence is angled at the same degree as the slope; and custom-building the fence so each paling touches the ground, creating a wavey line across the fence top and bottom.

Stepped Fencing

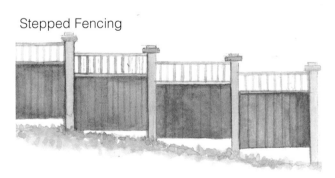

Sloped Fencing

Contour Fencing

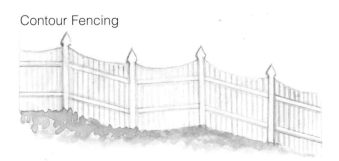

designing a **g**ate

The garden gate meets many needs, from practical to aesthetic to psychological. It is a place of romance—where else would an ardent suitor steal a kiss or wait for a late-night romantic tryst but by the garden gate?

On the purely practical side, a gate allows passage to and between a front and back garden. This functional aspect is closely tied to a gate's symbolic meaning. A locked, solid gate set in a high wall or fence provides a sense of privacy, enclosure, and security. A gate with an open design, even when set into a solid wall, has a welcoming air about it.

An open gate beckons; a tall, solid gate adds mystery, suggesting the entrance to a secret garden. It can guide the eye to a focal point or add charm, intimacy, drama, or panache.

Gates, even short ones that stand only 3 feet high, serve as important transition points from the garden to the outside world or from one part of the garden to another. They define boundaries while linking the two areas together. For that reason, gates and pathways tend to go together in a landscape design.

Don't confine your gates to the perimeter of your property. Use them within your garden as well, to divide space visually and to mark the boundaries between different areas or garden rooms.

Gates come in a seemingly endless variety of styles and sizes. Massive wrought-iron gates mark the entrances to many large Victorian parks and private estates. Painted, slatted gates set in white picket fences tend to belong with small, intimate cottages or traditional country homes. The gate to a vegetable plot at the bottom of the garden might be rough-hewn, in keeping with an untreated wooden fence designed to keep out foraging wildlife. Japanese moon gates have cutout circles symbolic of the full moon. These circles may be open or filled in with a fretted design of wood or iron to add visual interest and increase security.

Choose your gates to fit the style of your garden, but don't be afraid to have fun. For example, use a terra-cotta color to blend with a Spanish-style house, or set a light-colored gate set against a dark backdrop of heavy foliage.

HANGING A GATE

Battens

Temporary Post Support

Concrete

Gravel

Gate Latch

Hinge

1 Space the Posts. Lay the gate on the ground, and position the posts on each side, allowing enough space for the hinges and latch. Make sure the tops and bottoms of the posts are even. Nail temporary battens onto the posts as shown. (The bottom batten should be at the bottom of the gate.)

2 Set the Posts. Dig postholes. Set the posts on a gravel bed, making sure the bottom batten is 3 inches off the ground and that the posts are plumb and level. Secure the posts temporarily with braces and stakes, and then fill the holes with concrete. Check again for plumb and level before the concrete sets.

3 Hang the Gate. When the concrete has completely cured, remove the braces and battens, attach the hinges (with the gate attached) to the post, and then attach the latch. The job is easier if one person holds the gate in position while the other person drills the screw holes and attaches the hardware.

ABOVE LEFT Gates don't always need a fence. Here a decorative metal gate forms part of an arbor that is set in a hedge. This gate opens to a field beyond the garden.

ABOVE RIGHT Formal front yards require a distinctive-looking entrance. The metalwork shown here works well with the formal brick wall and posts topped with decorative urns.

BELOW LEFT This distinctive gate is attached to a house of similar style. Look to the facade of the house and the landscaping style of the front yard when selecting a fence and gate style.

BELOW RIGHT Informal designs put visitors at ease. This type of fence and gate is a good way to welcome visitors to a rear or side yard. It also helps support tall plants.

designing **a** **t**rellis

Trellises were a key element in Renaissance gardens and continued in popularity through the eighteenth century. Trellises enjoyed a resurgence of popularity in the late-nineteenth century, but never to the extent of earlier times.

Trellises can lend an air of magic and mystery to a garden. Generally we think of trellises in terms of the prefabricated sheets of diamond- or square-grid lattice and the fan-shaped supports for training climbers, both of which are readily available at home and garden centers in both wood and plastic. Lacking a pattern book, most gardeners are unaware of the incredible variety of designs, patterns, and optical illusions that can be created with trellises.

A trellis screen is a wonderfully airy way to achieve privacy or to partition off a space. The lath slats of lattice interrupt the view without totally obscuring it, creating the effect of a transparent curtain. Left bare, the pretty design of diamonds or squares makes an attractive effect. Covered in vines or decorated with hanging baskets, a trellis screen is enchanting.

The art of treillage, as the French call it, is not limited to screens. You can cover a bare wall or unattractive fence with a trellis pattern. Arrange the trellis pieces to create an optical illusion of an archway in the wall. Paint a realistic mural of the make-believe garden space beyond. Use a trellis for the walls of a gazebo to provide enclosure without being claustrophobic. Put a trellis screen with a pleasing, intricate pattern at the end of a walkway as a focal point.

TYPICAL TRELLIS DESIGNS

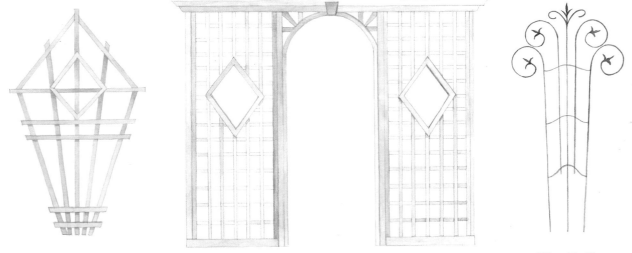

Traditional Wood Trellis   Trellis with Arched Entry   Wire Trellis

OPPOSITE TOP The simple lattice design of this fence is both appealing and practical. It not only encloses the garden but also serves as a trellis for climbing plants. A fence builder can create a custom design for you, or you can buy sections of fencing at home centers and fence speciality retailers.

OPPOSITE BOTTOM LEFT Closely spaced horizontal slats topped with decorative beams combine to form a handsome trellis and arbor that forms a border in this garden. The slats on the structure provide some privacy without impeding air flow into the garden. Decorative posts and beams add interest when seen from the street.

OPPOSITE BOTTOM RIGHT This arbor and trellis can serve as a destination in a large garden. You might find this type of structure in a front yard, but only in a very informal garden setting. Many large arbors contain a bench as part of the design. For interest, try placing a tall arbor in a rear or side yard that can be seen from the street.

designing arbors and pergolas

Far from being luxury items in the garden, arbors and pergolas can play a vital role in elevating the design and use of space from the ordinary to something special. The differences between an arbor and a pergola are somewhat technical, and you'll find people using the terms interchangeably. An arbor is a sheltered spot in which to sit. A pergola is generally a tunnel-like walkway or seating area created with columns or posts that support an open "roof" of beams or trelliswork. An arch (whether or not it has a curved top) is a structure through which you can walk.

Arches, arbors, and pergolas are stylish ways to mark the transition from one part of the garden to another. Place an arch or arbor around the gate into the garden or to mark the entrance from one garden "room" to another. Design the garden with reference to the arch or arbor so that the structure works as if it were a picture window, framing a vista or a pretty vignette. Another idea is to nestle an arbor on the edge of the property to give the illusion that there is a passageway to another section.

Arches, arbors, and pergolas must be connected to the overall design. For example, a path should lead to an arch or arbor. Place an arbor on the edge of the property, and then enhance the illusion that it is leading to additional grounds by camouflaging the property boundary with shrubs. Be sure to have a path leading to the arbor to anchor its position and to encourage people to stroll over and enjoy the haven it provides.

DETAILS FOR PERGOLA CONSTRUCTION

Post-and-Beam Pergola

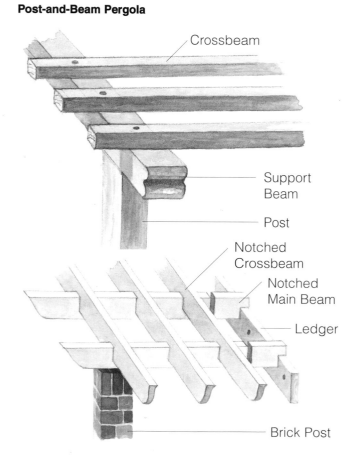

Crossbeam

Support Beam

Post

Notched Crossbeam

Notched Main Beam

Ledger

Brick Post

Pergolas should always be somewhat higher than they are wide. A minimum width of about 5 feet allows two people to walk through the pergola abreast. The structure should be high enough to allow a tall adult to walk underneath comfortably. The upright support posts also need to be in proportion to the roof. If the supports are hefty, the overhead beams also should be substantial. How far apart you space the roof beams depends on the final effect you want. Wide spacing creates a skylight effect. Close spacing makes the pergolas more tunnel-like.

ABOVE LEFT Draw attention to a walkway and the garden that flanks it by placing a decorative archway at the entrance. Structures such as this add a vertical element to the landscape design, and they serve to direct traffic along the path.

TOP RIGHT Stone and wood combine to form a distinctive landscape element. Structures such as this help to integrate the facade of the house with its surroundings.

ABOVE RIGHT While many entry arbors and archways have rounded tops, don't be afraid to experiment. The shape of this archway echoes the gables on the house beyond.

LEFT Although a well-designed arbor is beautiful in its own right, adding climbing roses or other flowering plants is a sure way to turn the structure into a focal point.

six "curb-appeal" designs

Before choosing any of the plantings suggested here, make sure they are compatible with your climate. The curved walk in the design, below, offers visitors a helpful "Please come this way." The first stage of the journey passes between two clipped shrub roses into a garden "room" with larger shrubs near the house and colorful perennials by the walk. An opening in a hedge of long-blooming shrub roses then leads to a wider paved area that functions as an outdoor foyer. There you can greet guests or relax on the bench and enjoy the plantings that open out onto the lawn. A double course of pavers intersects the walk and a planting bed, and the circle it describes contrasts nicely with the rectilinear lines of the house and hedge.

low-growing flair

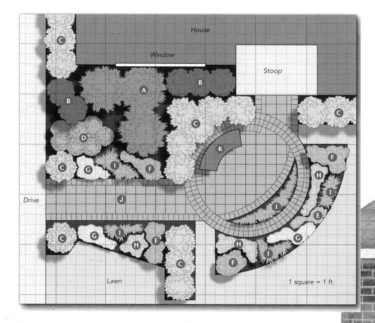

Plants and elements include 'Sea Green' juniper (A); dwarf cranberrybush viburnum(B); 'Frau Dagmar Hartop' rose (C); 'Little Princess' spirea (D); basket-of-gold (E); 'Goldsturm' black-eyed Susan (F); 'Moonbeam' coreopsis (G); 'Moonshine' yarrow (H); 'Stella d'Oro' daylily (I); a walk (J); and a bench (K).

USDA Hardiness Zones 3, 4, 5, 6

rosy, elegant entrance

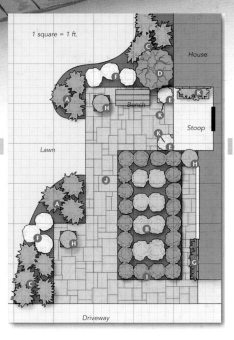

This simple arrangement of plants and paving produces an elegant entrance that deftly mixes formal and informal elements. A wide walk of neatly fitted flagstones and a rectangular bed of roses have the feel of a small formal courtyard, complete with a pair of "standard" roses in planters, each displaying a mound of flowers atop a single stem. Clumps of ornamental grass rise from the paving like leafy fountains.

Gently curving beds of low-growing evergreens and shrub roses edge the flagstones, softening the formality and providing a comfortable transition to the lawn. Morning glories and clematis climb simple trellises to brighten the walls of the house.

Flowers in pink, white, purple, and violet are abundant from early summer until frost. They are set off by the green foliage of the junipers and roses and the gray leaves of the catmint edging. Add a bench so you can linger and enjoy the scene; in later years, the star magnolia behind it will provide comfortable dappled shade.

Plants and elements include 'Blue Star' juniper (A); 'Bonica' rose (B); dwarf creeping juniper (C); star magnolia (D); 'The Fairy' rose (E); 'White Meidiland' rose (F); Jackman clematis (G); 'Gracillimus' Japanese silver grass (H); 'Six Hills Giant' catmint (I); flagstone paving (J); and planters (K).

USDA Hardiness Zones 4, 5, 6

a warm welcome

The ample bluestone walkway in this design invites visitors to stroll side by side through a small garden from the driveway to the entrance. The path is positioned to put the front door in full view of arriving guests. Its generous width allows for informal gatherings as guests arrive and depart, and well-chosen plants encourage lingering there to enjoy them.

Three small trees grace the entrance with spring and summer flowers, light shade, and superb fall color. Most of the perennials and shrubs are evergreen and look good year-round, providing a fine background to the flowers and an attractive foil to the fall color. In the winter, colorful tree bark and bright berries make gazing out the windows a pleasure.

Plants and elements include seviceberry (A); white evergreen azalea (B); 'Natchez' crape myrtle (C); 'Big Blue' lilyturf (D); 'Otto Luyken' cherry laurel (E); heavenly bamboo (F); Christmas rose (G); 'Blue Prince' holly (H); blue oat grass (I); a walkway (J); and stepping stones (K).

USDA Hardiness Zones 5, 6, 7

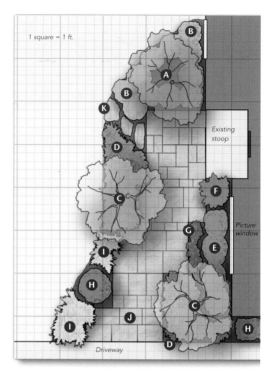

helpful hospitality ||||||||||||

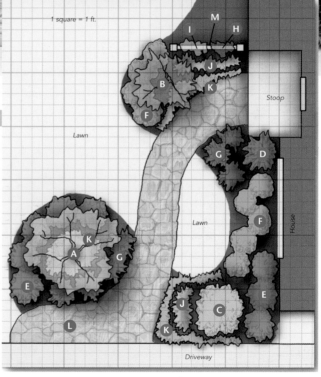

1 square = 1 ft.

Lawn

Lawn

House

Stoop

Driveway

The curved walkway in this design extends a helpful "Please come this way" to visitors while creating a roomy planting area near the house. The walk bridges a grassy "inlet" created by the free-flowing lines of the beds. The flowing masses of plants, lawn, and pavement nicely complement the journey to the front door.

Two handsome trees and a skirting of shrubs form a partial screen between the street and the walk and front door. A striking collection of evergreens transforms a foundation planting near the house into a shrub border. Ground covers edge the walkway with pretty foliage, flowers, and berries. A decorative screen by the stoop marks the entry. Fragrant flowers and colorful foliage cover the screen year-round, enticing visitors to linger awhile by the door.

The rest of the planting contributes to the all-season interest with flowers spring, summer, and fall (several fragrant). Colorful foliage and berries grace the autumn and winter months.

Plants and elements include river birch (A); Japanese maple (B); Burford holly (C); heavenly bamboo (D); 'Otto Luyken' cherry laurel (E); 'Helleri' Japanese holly (F); creeping willowleaf cotoneaster (G); Jackman clematis (H); Carolina jasmine (I); 'Stella d'Oro' daylily (J); creeping lilyturf (K); a walkway (L); and a screen (M).

USDA Hardiness Zones 6, 7, 8

simple style

In this design a flagstone walkway curves gracefully to the front door, creating a roomy planting bed near the house. Extending along the driveway, the paving makes it easier for passengers to get in and out of a car. Where the paving widens out at the front stoop, there's room for a welcoming bench sheltered by a small tree. Fragrant flowers and eye-catching foliage make the stroll to the door inviting, while providing interest to viewers inside the house and on the street.

The plants here are selected for a shady entry, one that gets less than six hours of sun a day. Flowers and foliage will keep the entry colorful and fragrant throughout the year. Redbud blossoms will join daffodils and dianthus in early spring, followed by columbine, plumbago, Mexican petunia, and gardenia. All but the gardenia continue to bloom well into fall. White daffodils and red camellias arrive in November and stay through the winter holidays.

Plants and elements include redbud (A); 'Daisy' gardenia (B); 'Yuletide' sasanqua camellia (C); dwarf yaupon holly (D); dwarf Mexican petunia (E); columbine (F); holly fern (G); tropical plumbago (H); 'Bath's Pink' dianthus (I); 'Ice Follies' daffodil (J); a walkway (K); and a bench (L).

USDA Hardiness Zones 6, 7, 8, 9

entryway with flair

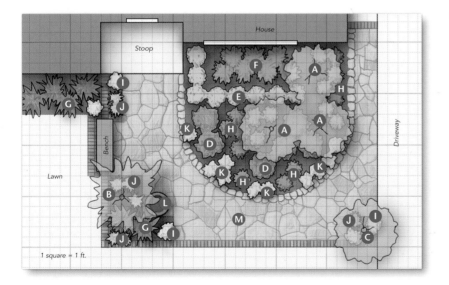

1 square = 1 ft.

The flagstone paving here creates a walkway with the feel of a cozy courtyard, an atmosphere enhanced by the small trees and bench. Extending along the driveway, the paving makes it easier for passengers to get in and out of a car. A semicircular garden makes the stroll to the door inviting, while providing interest to viewers inside the house and on the street.

Flowering trees and shrubs bloom throughout the spring and summer in pinks and lavenders. Attractive foliage, much of it evergreen, and striking bark ensure interest all year.

Plants and elements include 'Marina' arbutus (A); chaste tree (B); 'Zuni' crape myrtle (C); dwarf Indian hawthorn (D); 'Winter Gem' boxwood (E); purple fountain grass (F); 'Sundowner' New Zealand flax (G); 'Otto Quast' Spanish lavender (H); 'Sunset Gold' pink breath of heaven (I); blue oat grass (J); variegated lemon thyme (K); assorted annuals, such as a mix of pink, blue, and white salvia, lobelia, phlox, alyssum, and zinnia (L); and paving (M).

USDA Hardiness Zones 8, 9, 10

The exciting improvements you make to boost your home's curb appeal shouldn't disappear once the sun goes down. You can find a variety of outdoor lighting options that can add drama and play up your home's most interesting architectural and landscape features at night. There are also many attractive lighting options that can cover outdoor safety concerns after dark. At the minimum, you'll want to make sure that stairs, walkways, and the front entrance are adequately illuminated. But as the following pages show, there's a world of creative ideas that are practical and design-savvy.

Nightscaping

I architectural lighting I
I low-voltage lighting designs I

Evenly spaced light fixtures recessed into the soffits serve the dual purpose of illuminating this house and outlining the lines of its mid-century architecture.

Architectural lighting, also referred to as "accent lighting," is decorative. It's different from the type of lighting that is specifically for security. While architectural lighting may subtly illuminate dark stairways and paths, its main purpose is to create a play of light and shadow that can add drama to the exterior of your house after dark. Think about how you may have used accent lighting indoors to highlight a painting or an interesting architectural feature, for example. Then imagine how you can play up the most appealing exterior features of your house or the landscape. Often it's the architecture that merits major attention, but don't overlook the effects you can create by installing low-voltage fixtures within a bed of plantings or along a walkway. Or use a small spotlight to dramatize a large tree or statuary. Generally, your first goal should be to provide suitable light near the front door. Yet bright light, even there, is not necessary. The goal of outdoor lighting is not the intense illumination needed for tasks. In this chapter, you'll find ideas for the different types of effects you can create, as well as information about today's popular energy-efficient outdoor lighting systems. Keep in mind scale and proportion, balance, harmony, and rhythm. Don't focus light all in one spot. You can call for help from an exterior lighting specialist, but before you do, check out "Design Basics" on page 179. Many plans are fairly easy for do-it-yourselfers.

architectural lighting

OPPOSITE Thanks to well-placed downlights in the soffits and under the roof in the entry, the distinctive geometry and texture of the facade that distinguishes this house is as effective at night as it is during the day.

ABOVE A well-lit entry is the mainstay of this lighting scheme, yet note how the light that skims the wall of the house makes the texture palpable. Shadows created by uplighting plantings contribute to night interest, too.

RIGHT Special underwater lights make the fountain a focal point in this garden. Low-voltage lighting casts a soft glow on the arch that was inspired by classical architectural elements.

lighting effects

Vary lighting effects for maximum impact. *Uplighting* casts a pool of light upward. *Downlighting* does the opposite. Use them alone or together for contrast against a surface. Uplighting alone can provide fairly wide coverage of shrubbery in a border or against the foundation. Installed at the bottom of a tree, it can illuminate the upper branches. Downlighting alone is excellent for safety, and it's often used to brighten an entry and along paths and stairways. *Spotlighting* is more specific, casting a narrow beam of light on an object. Spotlighting is always done from a distance. To highlight something and eliminate shadows, you will have to light it from several directions. But if you choose to make use of the shadows and patterns created by light, try *backlighting*, which will project interesting silhouettes onto a surface.

To emphasize texture, such as that of a stone wall, a fence, grillwork, or foliage, lighting professionals use a technique called *grazing*. The fixture is placed close to the surface and aimed at a 45° angle. For an even wash of light, fixtures can be installed further away from the surface. This is referred to as *wall washing*.

Another technique, *moonlighting,* casts light down from several points in a tree.

ABOVE Uplighting within the foundation shrubbery beds and low-voltage fixtures scattered throughout add interest to this contemporary house.

LEFT A combination of fixtures makes the entryway the undeniable focal point in this nightscape. In addition to the pendant and wall-mounted lamps, recessed lighting in the garage roof's soffit accents a trellis and flower beds.

BELOW These stairs and landings are subtly but sufficiently illuminated.

ABOVE RIGHT These porches and side door have been amply lit for security and safety reasons.

BELOW RIGHT Beautiful architecture and tall palm trees deserve special attention here. A technique called grazing was used to direct light at an angle. This allows the fronds of the trees to cast evocative shadows on the walls. Uplighting the garden beds with low-voltage fixtures heightens the drama.

bright idea
specialty bulbs

A carbon-filament Victorian-style light bulb keeps a period design honest. Bulbs that imitate gaslights and flicker-flame bulbs can do it, but they cast very little light.

|||||| view your

LEFT If large windows are part of your home's design, nighttime lighting inside should be considered when you are devising an exterior lighting plan.

BELOW Both the interior and exterior lighting are the same crisp-white color of the house and in keeping with the architectural intent.

lighting design from inside and outside the house ||||||||||

big effects

Trees. The intricacies of tree branches, leaves, and even bark are particularly beautiful when bathed by light. To fully illuminate a tree, use a combination of lighting types. First, provide uplighting with a spotlight. Then try moonlighting. Place low-voltage downlighting fixtures in some of the high branches to make sure the tree doesn't wind up looking trunk heavy. It will also make leaves and branches reflect on the ground or a seating area below to create a lovely romantic effect.

Water Features. Carefully lit fountains, pools, ponds, and streams look magnificent in the night landscape. If you want to get creative, try a mirroring effect. Mirroring entails lighting a feature on the far side of a still body of water, such as an unlit pool, so that you can observe the mirrored image in the water. Another possibility is to install special submersible low-voltage lights inside your water feature.

Walls or Fencing. One way to accent a wall or fence is to wash it with light. This is a good idea if the color is really dramatic because it provides lots of even illumination so onlookers can see how color-savvy you are, day or night. Washing is also a good way to show off a great design.

RIGHT This glass-and-light effect looks spectacular against a dark night sky. When used selectively, light takes on shapes not unlike sleek modern architecture.

OPPOSITE TOP LEFT Windows aglow with soft interior light contribute to this night scheme. The sconce is purely an accent, but a fixture in the entry illuminates the door.

OPPOSITE TOP RIGHT Low-voltage lights built into the walls on either side of the stairs illuminate the way unobtrusively.

OPPOSITE BOTTOM Small strip lights line a walkway and steps in front of this home.

BELOW A pair of sconces make this semi-enclosed entry warm and welcoming at night. A ceiling-mounted fixture illuminates the front door. To the side, a lighted intercom and doorbell are easy to locate.

bright idea

spot on

Doorbells, security systems, and house numbers are available in lighted designs that are easy to see at night.

fixture styles and finishes

Outdoor lighting fixtures come in a variety of styles that allow you to provide light where you need it most and in ways that are effective and appealing. The choices range from standard lamppost fixtures, pendants, sconces, ceiling- and wall-mounted lamps, and floodlights to low-voltage lights for walkways, paths, stairs, and decorative effects, such as the ones that are discussed on page 168. You can easily find lighting fixtures to suit any house, from contemporary to colonial and other reproduction styles. Some of today's most popular design motifs are Arts and Crafts, Old World, Asian, Victorian, and mid-century modern. Numerous finishes include brass, chrome, stainless steel, wrought iron, nickel, copper, bronze, pewter, and verdigris. These finishes may be polished, brushed, oiled, antiqued, or weathered. Some styles mimic flowers, leaf patterns, acorns, or wildlife. Others resemble miniature pagodas. If you can't find what you need in a home center or a lighting store, search the Internet. This is also a good place to find one-of-a-kind or handcrafted fixtures that will add a unique note to your outdoor design efforts.

In addition to using fixtures that complement the style of your house, it's smart to coordinate these features with the hardware on your door. Although it's not important to match all of these items, it helps to create a harmonious look if you don't mix too many styles, colors, and finishes. In addition, if you're adding new fixtures to existing ones, you don't have to match them exactly if you choose a matching finish. It simply makes things easier than trying to coordinate different elements.

Most outdoor lighting has to be hard-wired. Low-voltage systems, as explained on pages 176-179, are fairly easy to install yourself. See "Design Basics" on page 179 for helpful information about where to install outdoor lights.

Another option is to use solar lights, which are energized by the sun so there is no wiring involved. However, you must install solar lights where they can get maximum direct sunlight—don't expect them to work in shaded areas. In addition, they are strictly decorative and don't generate an adequate level of light to brighten a walkway or stairs. Still, they are inexpensive and come in an array of styles, offering pizzazz for almost pennies.

bright idea

sensors and timers

For security, consider combining your outdoor lighting with devices that sense motion or operate off a timer-switch.

OPPOSITE BOTTOM LEFT This reproduction lantern fixture is called an "onion lamp." It's a style that originated in New England.

OPPOSITE BOTTOM CENTER This low-voltage fixture with a weathered rust finish comes with a mounting spike to keep it securely in the ground.

OPPOSITE BOTTOM RIGHT A solid traditional choice, this wall-mounted sconce has a wrought-iron finish.

RIGHT The repetitive use of the same-style fixture is a recognizable design element in its own right.

BELOW LEFT This pagoda-style lantern sits atop a stone wall. Its square shape suits the home's architectural features.

BELOW CENTER For occasional mood or party lighting, staked candle lanterns can direct guests to the scene or softly illuminate a pathway.

BELOW RIGHT A low-voltage lamp set on a timer draws evening attention to a bed of flowers.

low-voltage lighting

nstalling low-voltage lighting is one of the most popular do-it-yourself projects. Because the systems operate on only 12 volts of power as opposed to the 120 volts of standard line voltage, installing a low-voltage system is much safer than working on house wiring. Some manufacturers recommend turning on the power to connect the lights, so you can see the results right away. (Always follow the manufacturer's directions.)

Installation is easier, too. For most systems, all you have to do is plug in a step-down transformer to a standard GFCI-protected outdoor outlet and run the wires

OPPOSITE LEFT Small low-voltage spotlights set into the flower bed are directed upward to dramatize the branches of this massive tree.

OPPOSITE TOP RIGHT A low-voltage light in the popular mushroom design aims lighting down, pooling it to delineate a pathway or accent a flowerbed. The light spread by this kind of lamp can be up to 12 feet in diameter.

OPPOSITE BOTTOM RIGHT This polished-brass fixture in a traditional style is another type that complements pathways. In a design like this one, light is distributed evenly in a general direction rather than directed up or down.

RIGHT These lantern-style, low-voltage fixtures are suspended from posts resembling a shepherd's crook. They provide soft accent lighting along a pathway.

BELOW RIGHT This fixture is called a "well light." The housing is above-ground, and the light can be aimed in a specific direction. Another type of well light, one with a fixed beam, exposes only the lens and mounting ring to create a small disk of light on the ground.

designs

to the light fixtures. Working with low-voltage wiring means that there is no need to bury wires in conduit or as deeply as standard wiring. Requirements vary, but most manufacturers call for direct burial of a few inches.

The quick installation also means it's easy to alter the system by adding new fixtures or moving fixtures to new locations. That's a plus because landscapes tend to change over time, and a versatile low-voltage system can be redesigned to change with it.

the **r**ight **w**iring

Wire Gauge	Length of System (feet)	Maximum Wattage (watts)
16	100	150
14	150	200
12	200	250

design **b**asics

Survey your property. Identify the best locations for low-voltage lights. Note how moonlight affects the landscape. Examples include

▐ Highlighting focal points. Use lights to uplight a distinctive tree or shrub. Or train a floodlight on garden statuary or a water feature. It is best to choose no more than one or two focal points. Choosing too many will make the yard look chaotic.

▐ Lighting for safety. Fixtures installed along paths and driveways and on stairs add a measure of safety to your yard and outdoor living areas.

▐ Illuminating decks and patios. Low-voltage fixtures installed in deck railings or along the perimeter of patios provide good ambient lighting. They help extend the time these areas can be used.

Avoid mistakes. Don't over-light. Many homeowners make the mistake of installing too many lights, especially along walkways and driveways. Over-lighting in these areas creates an airport runway look, which is something to be avoided. Place fixtures so that they do not produce glare or shine into your home's windows or the windows of your neighbors.

Create a balanced lighting plan by varying the lighting techniques. For example, try teaming a dramatically uplighted tree with subtle walkway lighting that casts small pools of light.

Pick a system. You will find it helpful to sketch your lighting plan on paper. The perspective a scaled drawing affords you makes it easy to make changes quickly.

Once you have a plan, choose the fixtures you want to use. Home centers and lighting stores usually have a selection of fixtures and low-voltage systems in stock. Lighting kits often contain everything you will need. The disadvantage is limited fixture selection. Fixtures that will be visible should look as attractive during the day as they do when they are illuminated at night.

Wiring. When assembling components for low-voltage lighting, determine the length of the wiring runs. This will tell you what gauge wiring to buy. Unlike line-voltage lights, low-voltage lights experience a drop-off in power the farther away the light fixture is from the transformer, so matching the right wiring to the system is important. Follow manufacturer's recommendations.

Accessories. One of the most practical accessories for a low-voltage system is a mechanism for activating and turning off the lights. Many systems are light-sensitive, meaning that they turn on at dusk and off at dawn. An alternative is a system that switches on at dusk and then remains on for a predetermined number of hours.

OPPOSITE LEFT The cables used for fixtures like these can be buried underground for the sake of tidiness. But if you're thinking of rearranging the system, it's safe to leave the cables aboveground.

▐

ABOVE Light fixtures installed in steps make this deck safer. When designing similar lights for your stairs, make sure the lights do not cause glare.

▐

OPPOSITE RIGHT These solar-powered lights are easy to install; they work on batteries that are charged by the sun's energy.

An unusual vase, wall art, or a kitschy flea-market find—many people know how to accent the rooms inside their homes using objects such as these to complement their interior design. But few people think to accessorize the living area outside the front door. A few well-chosen items, from small furniture to unique artwork, can add your signature—and lots of curb appeal—to the rest of your design plan for the front of your house. Try to use things that say something about you and your family or decorative items that accentuate your home's style. Here are some ideas.

Accents and Accessories

| personality plus |

Create an outdoor designscape next to the door or on a front terrace or porch by grouping items like these clay pots and fresh flowering plants from your garden.

bright idea

outside art

Leave the Picasso inside, and look for inexpensive paintings or prints to decorate a sheltered outdoor wall.

ABOVE LEFT Even a practical item such as a doormat can show off your style. Personalize it with a monogram.

ABOVE RIGHT Stone urns, like this one filled with fruit, add a formal note to a front garden. Some urns can be filled with plants or flowers so that you change your theme with the seasons. If stone is too expensive, substitute with affordable look-alikes made of polystyrene.

LEFT Any covered ledge or flat surface is an excellent place for a display of pretty items, from flowerpots to seashells.

OPPOSITE Bold blue paint makes a big statement on this privacy wall and creates a backdrop for Majolica and other pottery as well as an antique metal bench. The colorful Mexican pillow adds a perfect accent.

There are many ways to put your unique stamp on the appearance of your home. One of the least expensive and easiest is accessorizing. If you think you need to be a decorator to add a few extra finishing touches, get over it. Anyone who can claim a favorite color or an interest in life can come up with something decorative to display. Start by looking for things you like—not what you think is trendy or something you've seen at friends' places or the neighbor's house. Take time to scout around to find unusual things. Shop antique stores, on-line retailers, art shows, flea markets, even garage sales. Then when you've gathered your treasures, play with different ways to arrange them to give them impact. Don't forget to add color when you have an opportunity, especially if the house is a neutral or earth tone hue. And remember to choose items that can withstand the elements.

personality plus

accessorize with everyday items

Purchasing decorative items, especially those that are one-of–a-kind, can get costly. Instead, try shopping around in your attic, basement, or garage. Look at old items that you may have stashed away because you've redecorated. Perhaps a pillow or throw that no longer suits your family room is the thing needed to make your porch furniture extra cozy. Vintage items often have whimsical appeal. They might include an old wagon, bicycle, or milk box, advertising signs, even your granddad's gardening tools. Any of these types of things can be organized and displayed to advantage. Don't overlook a tattered item's potential. For example, you may not have the refinishing skills to make an old side table suitable for indoor use, but you could easily paint it and put it outside for decorative purposes. A milk box may not look like much, but if you stencil your name and house number on it and fill it with a cascading plant, it becomes a unique accent outside the front door. Some other things you could do include spray-painting an old birdcage and filling it with flowers; decorating scrap wood with a favorite quote or saying and displaying it in a flower bed; recycling colorful bottles and jars and using them to hold candles; refinishing clay pots and planters with mosaic tiles made from shards of broken china; stringing miniature holiday lights in trees or on a fence or trellis; and using chipped or cracked cups or teapots as small planters.

OPPOSITE A beat-up bentwood chair minus its seat has become a lovely planter. Nestled among other planters, it is the signature piece in this vignette.

ABOVE This artful topiary needs regular trimming to keep its shape, but it's surely a unique conversation piece.

ABOVE RIGHT Mix-and-match pieces are always more interesting than matched sets. These look at home in this small sitting area. The decking, which has been painted bright blue, anchors the space with personality.

RIGHT It's been said that art imitates life. In this case, it imitates a plush conversation spot. These sandstone pieces furnish a front patio.

even small touches make a house stand out

OPPOSITE TOP LEFT This Victorian iron plant stand is perfect for a lush Boston fern. Salvaged architectural and garden ornaments are terrific items for outdoor decorating.

OPPOSITE TOP RIGHT Birdhouses and the creatures they attract are always charming accessories to a front garden.

RIGHT A swag created with fresh greenery and accented with colorful fruit is a lovely way to accessorize around the door. Create an outline of the area you plan to fill. Cut a piece of plywood to the desired size and shape. Hammer nails through the board from back to front, and affix greenery and fruit to the protruding nails.

OPPOSITE BOTTOM LEFT In the spirit of everyday items, garden tools, a collection of canes, and even an old tackle basket can be grouped in ways that make a pleasing picture.

OPPOSITE BOTTOM RIGHT Small details go the distance when it comes to personalizing space. Here, a pineapple knocker embodies the spirit of welcome.

RIGHT Furniture and small items look homey on this shady porch.

OPPOSITE Water features are particularly soothing. This pond is at the center of a front garden. Small statuary has been placed along its edge.

BELOW LEFT This authentic Victorian lawn roller looks elegant propped against a tree in the front yard. It's a fine example of a practical object of another era that has enough style to be considered decorative today.

RIGHT A beautiful fountain can be admired for its visual appeal as well as the comforting sound of moving water that it provides.

BELOW RIGHT Stepping-stones like these allow you to lead the eye to any part of the property you want in focus. They also make perfect secondary pathways to different areas, such as an arbor or a front-yard terrace.

Resource Guide

MANUFACTURERS

Andersen Windows
100 Fourth Ave., N
Bayport, MN 55003
800-426-4261
www.andersenwindows.com
Manufactures windows and doors, and accessories for them.

Artcrete
5812 Hwy. 494
Natchitoches, LA 71457
318-379-2000
www.artcrete.com
Manufactures Faux Brick® Stenciled Concrete.

Atlas Homewares
326 Mira Loma Ave.
Glendale, CA 91204
818-240-3500
www.atlashomewares.com
Manufactures house numbers, door knockers, and doorbells.

Baldwin Hardware Corp.
841 E. Wyomissing Blvd.
Reading, PA 19611
800-566-1986

www.baldwinhardware.com
Manufactures locks and door hardware.

Behr
3400 W. Segerstrom Ave.
Santa Ana, CA 92704
877-237-6158
www.behr.com
Manufactures paint.

Benjamin Moore & Co.
51 Chestnut Ridge Rd.
Montvale, NJ 07645
201-573-9600
www.benjaminmoore.com
Manufactures paint.

Bomanite
232 S. Schnoor Ave.
Madera, CA 93637
559-673-2411
www.bomanite.com
Manufactures architectural concrete paving and flooring material.

C & S Distributors, Inc.
1640 Rte. 5
South Windsor, CT 06074
800-842-7307

The following list of manufacturers and associations is meant to be a general guide to additional industry and product-related sources. It is not intended as a listing of products and manufacturers represented by the photographs in this book.

www.c-sdistributors.com

Provides building supplies for building and remodeling projects.

CertainTeed

800-782-8777

www.certainteed.com

Manufactures roofing materials, siding, windows, and fence, deck, and rail components.

Clopay Building Products

8585 Duke Blvd.

Mason, OH 45040

www.clopay.com

Manufactures residential garage doors.

Devoe Paint

East Building

15885 W. Sprague Rd.

Strongsville, OH 44136

440-297-8635

www.devoepaint.com

Manufactures interior and exterior paint.

Dutch Boy

800-828-5669

www.dutchboy.com

Manufactures interior and exterior paint.

GAF Materials Corp.

1361 Alps Rd.

Wayne, NJ 07470

973-628-3000

www.gaf.com

Manufactures roofing materials.

Garden Supply Co.

1421 Old Apex Rd.

Cary, NC 27513

919-460-7747

www.gardensupplyco.com

A source for plants, including annuals, perennials, trees, and shrubs, and garden complements, such as fountains, statuary, and garden art.

GardenWeb

www.gardenweb.com

Offers seed and plant exchanges, plant reference guides, and links to shopping sites.

Gerkin Windows & Doors

P.O. Box 3203

Sioux City, IA 51102

800-475-5061

www.gerkin.com

Manufactures aluminum windows, storm doors, vinyl windows, and patio doors.

Resource Guide

Hooks & Lattice
5671 Palmer Way, Ste. K
Carlsbad, CA 92010
800-896-0978
www.hooksandlattice.com
Manufactures window boxes and planters.

Intermatic, Inc.
Intermatic Plaza
Spring Grove, IL 60081
815-675-7000
www.intermatic.com
Manufactures lighting products, including low-voltage lighting systems.

James Hardie Siding Products
26300 La Alameda, Ste. 250
Mission Viejo, CA 92691
888-542-7343
www.jameshardie.com
Manufactures fiber-cement siding, backerboard, and pipe.

Jeld-Wen, Inc.
P.O. Box 3203
Sioux City, IA 51102
800-535-3936
www.jeld-wen.com
Manufactures windows, exterior doors, patio doors, and garage doors in numerous styles and sizes.

Kwikset Corp.
19701 DaVinci
Lake Forest, CA 92610
800-327-5625
www.kwikset.com
Manufactures residential locksets and door hardware.

Mark Tirondola
40 Pidretti Ct.
Bloomfield, NJ 07003
973-338-5403
www.tirondolapainting.com
Provides painting services.

Marvin Windows and Doors
P.O. Box 100
Warroad, MN 56763
888-537-7828
www.marvin.com
Manufactures windows and swinging and sliding doors.

Monier Lifetile
P.O. Box 19792
Irvine, CA 92623
209-982-1473
www.monierlifetile.com
Manufactures roof tiles of various weights and styles.

Nightscaping

1705 E. Colton Ave.

Redlands, CA 92374

800-544-4840

www.nightscaping.com

Manufactures professional outdoor lighting.

Park Seed Company

1 Parkton Ave.

Greenwood, SC 29647

800-213-0076

www.parkseed.com

Offers plant seeds, bulbs, and gardening supplies.

Pella Windows & Doors

102 Main St.

Pella, IA 50219

www.pella.com

Manufactures windows and exterior doors.

Pratt and Lambert Paints

800-289-7728

www.prattandlambert.com

Manufactures paint.

Restoration Hardware

800-910-9836

www.restorationhardware.com

Manufactures indoor and outdoor furniture, windows, and lighting accessories.

Salsbury Industries

1010 E. 62nd St.

Los Angeles, CA 90001

www.mailboxes.com

Manufactures residential mailboxes.

Schlage Lock Co.

1010 Sante Fe St.

Olathe, KS 66051

888-805-9837

www.schlage.com

Manufactures locksets.

Stoett Industries, Inc.

1234 Integrity Dr.

Defiance, OH 43512

419-784-0030

www.stoett.com

Manufactures retractable screens and retractable screen doors.

Therma-Tru Doors

1750 Indian Wood Circle

Maumee, OH 43537

800-843-7628

www.thermatru.com

Manufactures fiberglass exterior doors.

Resource Guide

The Scotts Company

14111 Scottslawn Rd.

Marysville, OH 43041

888-270-3714

www.scotts.com

Offers lawn and garden products.

The Sherwin-Williams Company

101 Prospect Ave., NW

Cleveland, OH 44115

800-4 SHERWIN

www.sherwin-williams.com

Manufactures paint.

Timberlane Woodcrafters, Inc.

197 Wissahickon Ave.

North Wales, PA 19454

800-250-2221

www.timberlane.com

Manufactures exterior wood shutters.

Valspar Corporation

1191 Wheeling Rd.

Wheeling, IL

800-845-9061

www.valspar.com

Manufactures paint.

Your Color Source Studios, Inc.

67 Gates Ave.

Montclair, NJ 07042

973-509-2304

www.yourcolorsource.com

Provides color consulting services.

AGENCIES & ASSOCIATIONS

Energy Star

1200 Pennsylvania Ave., NW

Washington, DC 20460

888-782-7937

www.energystar.gov

Energy Star provides programs and products designed to save energy.

National Association of the Remodeling Industry (NARI)

800-611-NARI

www.nari.org

An organization of contractors, remodelers, subcontractors, and design-build firms that offers education, tips, and a referral service to consumers.

The American Institute of Architects (AIA)

1735 New York Ave., NW

Washington, DC 20006

800-242-3837

www.aia.org

A national professional organization for licensed architects. Local chapters offer a referral service to consumers.

The American Society of Landscape Architects (ASLA)

636 Eye St., NW

Washington, DC 20001

202-898-2444

www.asla.org

A national professional organization of landscape architects.

Glossary

Accent lighting: A type of light that highlights an area or object to emphasize it.

Acrylic: A water-based plastic polymer that acts as the binder in acrylic paints.

Aggregate: Crushed stone, gravel, or other material added to cement to make concrete or mortar. Gravel and crushed stone are considered coarse aggregate; sand is considered fine aggregate.

Alkyd paints: Paints with artificial resins (alkyds) forming the binder often imprecisely called "oil-based" paints. Alkyds have replaced the linseed oil formerly used as a binder in paints that are oil-based.

Arbor: An arched, open structure that spans a doorway or provides shelter for a seat. Often covered with vines and used as a garden focal point.

Arch: An upright support structure for vines or climbing plants, often used to mark an entry or transition area in a garden.

Art Nouveau style: A late nineteenth-century style that was based on natural forms. It was the first style to reject historical references and create its own design vocabulary, which includes styled curved details.

Arts and Crafts style: A style that evolved during the late nineteenth century until about 1910 out of rebellion against the overly ornate Victorian style. It features a low-pitched gable roof and wide overhanging eaves and is often one-and-one-half stories high with decorative beams under the gables. It is also called Craftsman style.

Backfill: To fill in an area, such as a planting hole, trench, or around a foundation, using soil or gravel.

Backlighting: Illumination coming from a source behind or at the side of an object.

Base map: A drawing or survey that details the location of all property boundaries, structures, slopes, significant

plantings, and location of sunrise and sunset.

Berm: A mound of earth that directs or retains water. A 6-inch berm built around the drip line of a tree or shrub will create a basin, ensuring that water reaches the roots.

Cape Cod style: A modest symmetrical style, with a door in the center, that evolved in New England during the late 1700s. It features a steep roof with a slight overhang, may be one or one-and-one-half stories high, or may have dormers.

Casement window: A window that consists of one framed-glass panel that is hinged on the side. It swings outward from the opening at the turn of a crank.

Code: A locally or nationally enforced mandate regarding structural design, materials, plumbing, or electrical systems that states what you can or cannot do when building or remodeling. Codes are intended to protect standards of health, safety, and land use.

Colonial style: A house with the square symmetrical architecture that evolved out of the Neoclassical English Georgian style and was typical of the early eighteenth century. True Colonials also feature a pediment or crown molding above the front door, side windows that flank the door, and paired chimneys.

Color scheme: A group of colors used

together to create visual harmony.

Color wheel: A pie-shaped diagram showing the range and relationships of colors to one another.

Complementary colors: Colors located opposite one another on the color wheel.

Contrast: Colors with different values and intensities that create harmony together within a color scheme.

Cool colors: Blue, green, and violet.

Craftsman style: See *Arts & Crafts style*.

Dimmer switch: A switch that can vary the intensity of the light source that it controls.

Double-hung window: A window that consists of two framed-glass panels that slide open vertically, guided by a metal or wood track.

Downlighting: A lighting technique that illuminates areas or objects from above.

Earth tones: The natural colors of the earth; brown, beige, and some shades of green.

Federal style: A Neoclassical style that was popular after 1780 until about 1840. Symmetrical like the English Georgian and American Colonial styles before it, Federal style popularized patriotic motifs, such as eagles, swags, and garlands. Architec-

turally, a Federal-style building features a low-pitched roof or a flat roof with a balustrade, moldings, a fanlight over the front door, and sidelights.

Fixed window: A window that cannot be opened. It is usually a decorative unit, such as a half-round or Palladian-style window.

Footprint: The perimeter of a house or other significant structure, shown on a property survey.

Gothic Revival style: A mid-nineteenth-century style that drew inspiration from the medieval period. A Gothic-Revival building features a steeply pitched roof, grouped chimneys, pointed arches, and quatrefoils, such as clover-shaped windows.

Greek Revival style: A style that drew inspiration from ancient Greece. Its motifs include the Greek key and acanthus, and classical elements, such as columns and decorative pilasters. It most cases, the front entry of a Greek Revival building features a gable with a pediment and side columns.

Ground-fault circuit interrupter (GFCI): A safety circuit breaker that compares the amount of current entering a receptacle with the amount leaving. If there is a discrepancy of 0.005 volt, the GFCI breaks the circuit in a fraction of a second. GFCIs are required by the National Electrical Code in areas that are subject to dampness.

Glossary

Grout: A binder and filler applied in the joints between ceramic tiles.

Halogen bulb: A bulb filled with halogen gas, a substance that causes the particles of tungsten to be redeposited onto the tungsten filament. The function extends the lamp's life and makes the light whiter and brighter.

Hardscape: Parts of a landscape constructed from materials other than plants, such as walks, walls, and trellises made of wood, stone, or other materials.

Hue: A synonym for color.

Incandescent lamp: A lamp that contains a conductive filament through which current flows. The current reacts with an inert gas inside the bulb, which makes the filament glow.

Indirect lighting: A subdued type of lighting that is not head on, but reflected.

Italianate style: This style was most popular in America between 1860 and the late 1870s. It was inspired by Italian Renaissance country villas and features a symmetrical facade, low or pitched roof, and overhanging eaves. Italianate buildings often have a square cupola, balustraded balconies, and tall narrow windows.

Intensity: When describing attributes of a color, the strength in terms of brightness or dullness. Also referred to as a color's purity or saturation.

International style: A style of architecture that evolved after World War I that features a flat roof, casement windows, and a smooth, unornamented surface.

Latex paints: Paints that contain acrylic or vinyl resins, or a combination of the two. High-quality latex paints contain 100-percent acrylic resin. Latex paints are water-soluble; that is, they can be thinned and cleaned up with water.

Low-voltage lights: Lights that operate on 12 to 50 volts rather than the standard 120 volts for residential use.

Muntins: Framing members of a window that divide the panes of glass.

Palette: A range of colors that complement one another.

Parterre: Diminutive hedges, such as boxwood, used to divide space and serve as decorative frames for the plantings in formal gardens.

Pergola: A tunnel-like walkway or seating area with columns or posts to support an open "roof" of beams or trelliswork; usually covered with vines.

Plat: Prepared by professional surveyors, a plat shows precise property lines and any easements. It is used for making a base map for landscaping and is available from a tax assessor's office or given to homeowners when they purchase their property.

Prairie style: An architectural style designed by Frank Lloyd Wright between 1900 and 1920 that features a low-pitched roof, wide overhanging eaves, a central chimney, and rows of small windows.

Proportion: The relationship of one object to another.

Ranch style: A single-story rectangular, L- or U-shaped house.

Recessed light fixtures: Light fixtures that are installed in soffits or ceilings and are flush with the surrounding area.

Roof window: A horizontal window that is installed on the roof.

Scale: The size of an area or object.

Sconce: A type of light fixture that features a decorative metal wall bracket and glass housing, which shields a bulb.

Sliding window: Similar to a double-hung window turned on its side. The glass panels slide horizontally.

Snap-in grilles: Ready-made rectangular and diamond-pattern grilles that snap into a window sash and create the look of a true divided-light window.

Softscape: The palette of plants used in a landscape.

Split-level style: A variation on the ranch style, the split-level style evolved during the 1930s. It features an asymmetrical appearance, two stories, and an attached garage. Variations on the style include the bi-level and raised ranch.

True divided-light window: A window composed of multiple glass panes that

are divided by and held together by muntins.

Victorian style: A style that was first popularized between 1840 and 1904. It features an asymmetrical facade, a steeply pitched roof, a front-facing gable, and a porch.

Warm colors: Red, yellow, orange, and brown.

Zones: Climate divisions on a map indicating extreme cold or heat for that area, used to determine a plant's suitability. Also refers to divisions of a garden.

Index

Index

Index

Photo and